MW01625266

# CANADA'S RABBI:
# THE LIFE AND LEGACY OF RABBI REUVEN BULKA

# Canada's Rabbi

## *The Life and Legacy of Rabbi Reuven Bulka*

הרב ראובן פנחס ע"ה

*by*

Rikki (Bulka) Ash

Ktav Publishing House

CANADA'S RABBI: THE LIFE AND LEGACY OF RABBI REUVEN BULKA

KTAV PUBLISHING HOUSE
527 Empire Blvd
Brooklyn, NY 11225
www.ktav.com
orders@ktav.com
Ph: (718) 972-5449 / Fax: (718) 972-6307
ISBN 978-1-60280-502-6

Set in Arno Pro by Raphaël Freeman MISTD, Renana Typesetting

# Contents

*In eternal gratitude to the guiding light of our grandparents, present and forever cherished.*

*To Sabba a"h and Savta a"h, Grandma and Grandpa, and Bubbie Leah.*

*To Bubby and Zeidy Lew and Savta and Saba Ash a"h.*

# Foreword

I can't remember the exact circumstances when I first met Rabbi Bulka. But what I've never forgotten is that by the time he left the room, everyone was smiling.

Many years ago, I was working at a radio station in Ottawa and Rabbi Bulka was a frequent guest and regular weekend host. On his way into the studio, he would pass through the newsroom, say hello to everyone, make a few quips, and hand out candy. And no matter how depressing the news, or how much stress the staff felt about meeting deadlines, the room was always a little brighter after he left.

It was the same thing when we appeared on the air together. I could barely introduce him as a guest before he would jump in with a joke or tell a funny story. We would proceed to have a thoughtful conversation about a very serious topic. And then he would end with another amusing anecdote. Every time, I felt happier.

After one on-air conversation, I thought to myself, "Why can't everyone be like Rabbi Bulka?" He made it look so easy.

Every December, we would host a day-long fundraising show called the Christmas Cheer Broadcast. Even though he didn't celebrate Christmas, he participated enthusiastically. It seemed like he was at every event in Ottawa. And he was also everyone's spiritual advisor, even if they weren't members of his congregation or even Jewish.

We shared many things, including a love of baseball. One spring night I was out at an event and as I walked back to my car, I noticed the bright lights of a neighbourhood[1] ballpark. I wandered over to watch

1. AUTHOR'S NOTE: The majority of the text in this book adheres to American

for a minute and I saw Rabbi Bulka pitching a softball to someone on the other team. He was probably in his early 60s at the time, but he was enjoying himself thoroughly.

It was from Rabbi Bulka that I first learned about Viktor Frankl. I attended a workshop during which he talked about Frankl's life and lessons, including his greatest insight: that we have the option to choose how we react to events in our lives. It resonated with me like nothing else I've ever heard. I read as much as I could about Frankl, including some of what Rabbi Bulka had written, and I vowed to be mindful of the choices I was making whenever I was faced with difficult circumstances. Even when something angered or frustrated or threatened me, I still chose my response. As I once discussed with Rabbi Bulka, there's great responsibility in that message, but also great freedom.

And he didn't just talk about Viktor Frankl's message, he modeled it. Rabbi Bulka chose how he reacted to everything he experienced. He never grumbled, even when his wife was sick with cancer. I never saw him in a bad mood. And he never wore a coat, even on the coldest winter days in Ottawa. I guess he chose not to be cold.

Frankl's message was the root of some of the Rabbi's most important work. He launched an initiative that would resonate throughout our city, all based on a simple idea: Let's choose to be kind. He launched Kindness Week with the goal of encouraging random acts of kindness. He inspired people not only to be kind, but to share what they were doing.

I'm sure there were some people who rolled their eyes at the idea, thinking it was corny or idealistic. But it worked. People started registering their acts of kindness. And you heard stories about people helping each other, or buying a coffee for a stranger, or making an

---

English conventions. However, when quoting or sharing content written by Canadian sources, I have retained the original Canadian English spelling and style to preserve the authenticity and context of the material. This approach ensures that the contributions of Canadian authors and sources remain faithful to their intended presentation while maintaining consistency throughout the book.

extra effort to brighten someone's day. Even one act of kindness can change a person's day. Imagine what a thousand acts can do for an entire community.

In the chapters that follow, you'll learn how Rabbi Bulka embraced a life filled with profound meaning and unwavering kindness, leaving an indelible mark on Ottawa, Canada, and the world. You will discover the remarkable impact of the actions of an incredible man, whose example continues to inspire and uplift many lives.

Rabbi Bulka chose kindness, over and over. He chose to invest in kindness like it was an annuity that could generate returns for years to come.

When he was facing his own devastating diagnosis and he knew the end of his life was near, Rabbi Bulka agreed to do an interview for my podcast. In it, he shared a lifetime's worth of wisdom. He talked about leading by example, finding purpose in life, embracing uncertainty, and being aware of your own ego. And he shared another lesson I haven't forgotten. I asked him what it takes to be a good leader. "Instead of saying I'm the ultimate problem-solver who will make things good for everyone, listen, listen, listen. That's the most important thing."

Rabbi Bulka inspired me to take accountability for my reactions, to make better choices, to try harder to serve my community. I wish I could have spoken to him when I decided to run to be mayor of Ottawa, but I applied his lessons throughout the process and during the campaign. I still hear his voice when I need it.

I miss our conversations. I miss seeing him around the community. But I think of him every time I have an opportunity to be kind. That, above everything else, is Rabbi Bulka's legacy.

Mark Sutcliffe<br>
Mayor of Ottawa<br>
2024

# Preface

The circumstances surrounding this book are not easy. Publicized to the world on January 10, 2021, Rabbi Bulka, my grandfather, was diagnosed with pancreatic cancer that had unfortunately already metastasized to the liver.

As soon as his diagnosis went public, the outpouring of messages and love was incredible and extensive. Few people in the world receive 1,000 emails in one day, none of them spam, and all of them with words of encouragement and broken-heartedness.

I had always toyed with the idea of writing a book about my grandfather's extraordinary life, but every time I suggested it, my grandfather rejected the suggestion due to his high level of humility. After his diagnosis, he finally agreed to let me write this book and I was fortunate to spend hours speaking with and interviewing him about many aspects of his life.

Back in 2016, after I gave a class on the *Shemoneh Esreh* (a central prayer in Jewish Liturgy), my grandfather asked me if I wanted to co-author a book with him on the topic. I was ecstatic at the opportunity, as writing was something I had always enjoyed, and the opportunity to work with my grandfather on such a project was a dream come true. I can now admit that I didn't contribute much to the book. I wrote my own introduction, made some additions and edits, but it was by and large my grandfather's book that he allowed me the privilege of working on with him, although he would tell you that I did a lot more. I recall going to the local sushi restaurant in Lawrence,

New York, writing a lot of the book on napkins, as we had somehow forgotten to bring a notebook. It was a very special moment when our book was released, and I know my grandfather was very proud to have worked on it with me.

Fast forward to 2021, and I had grown up quite a bit in the previous five years. I had become a wife and mother in that time and had four years of teaching high school under my belt. When my grandfather was diagnosed, he was in the middle of writing a book entitled *Fixing Tikkun Olam*. I was honored when he asked me to edit it after it became evident that he wouldn't be able to do so himself. Having already worked with Rabbi Bulka on a previous book and read through much of his literature, I had a sense of his writing style and was able to edit it, hopefully to his liking.

It is humbling to have been called his "co-author" and editor, but I must say that being his "biographer" is a much more daunting endeavor.

For one thing, although I initially interviewed my grandfather for this book, he is no longer here for follow-up questions, for ideas of how to phrase certain points, for the countless times I almost pick up the phone to call him before I realize that I will forever only reach his voicemail.

There is not one single person who would be able to tell me all of the things my grandfather did for his community throughout his lifetime, including my grandfather himself. In order to get even a small picture of what his life was dedicated to, it took interviewing multitudes of friends, family members and colleagues and listening to countless stories during the week of *Shiva* and beyond. I'm not sure how many grandchildren can say that they learned new things about their grandparents with a google search, but that has proven true throughout the research for this book. Even so, there is no way I will be able to do his life justice.

As much as I'd like to tie up this book with a neat, perfect bow and say I have left no stone unturned, that would border on "closure," a term Rabbi Bulka always met with disdain (See appendix for a partial list of the words and sayings that Rabbi Bulka disliked – there were many.) Rabbi Bulka never believed in the idea of closure. And truth be told, there are multitudes of books that could be written about his life. So, consider this a taste of who Rabbi Bulka was, with the door left open for more.

# Introduction

Rabbi Bulka was renowned for his incorporation of Judaism and psychology at a time when they were seldom joined in tandem. Beginning with Rabbi Bulka's thesis on logotherapy and religion in 1971, closely followed by his founding of *The Journal of Psychology and Judaism*, these two disciplines were the subject of over 30 works that Rabbi Bulka authored.

When Rabbi Bulka was looking to study psychology, Judaism, and religion at the University of Ottawa, a professor asked him if he had ever heard of a "Viktor Frankl." When Rabbi Bulka replied that he had not, the professor suggested he might be interested. Rabbi Bulka bought his latest book and thought, "It was incredible, it's almost as if this fellow has been inside the mindset of Jewish religious leaders over the generations and has figured out a way to amalgamate it into a psychological system".[1]

My grandfather was desperate to get in touch with Frankl. He recalled:

> I called the publisher in New York, and they said we don't give out his address, but you can send us a letter and we'll send it to him. So, I sent him a letter through the publisher. A few months later, I'm sitting in the kitchen and the phone rings. In those days, the operator announces who is on the other end: "Frankl from Europe calling." I had no idea who this is. Turns

1. Noetic Films, "Reuven Bulka on Viktor Frankl," YouTube video, posted May 13, 2020, https://www.youtube.com/watch?v=f4C4j9vX4ac.

> out it was Dr. Viktor Frankl himself. He was calling to tell me he was coming to America and that if I have time, I could go to meet him. I was in the middle of my studies, so I said, "Great, where are you going to be?" He said he would be in Rochester, New York, which is about a five-hour drive from Ottawa. He warned me he was on a very tight schedule, and he would only have five minutes for me.[2]
>
> "So, I got into the car and drove all the way out to Rochester and we meet and I'm looking at the clock and seeing I have five minutes and I need to be careful because what am I going to say in five minutes? And it turns out we spent the better part of an entire afternoon and evening together. Five minutes turned out to be four hours. And that was the most lasting impression that to this very day I have of a person that valued his time but who spent it so liberally when it was for something that he felt was meaningful."

Clearly, it was meaningful enough that the relationship between Frankl and my grandfather evolved to the point where Frankl requested that, when the day would arrive, Rabbi Bulka come to Vienna to preside at his funeral. When he later passed away in 1997, Frankl was buried too quickly for my grandfather to fulfill his promise. In the end, my grandfather presided over a ceremony at the cemetery.

It is gratifying to know that the figurehead of the "meaning movement" found so much meaning in a relationship with my grandfather. As Rabbi Bulka's granddaughter, I can relate. One of the many side benefits of writing this book was the opportunity I had to connect with Dr. Frankl's own grandson, Alex Vesely, who is actively furthering his grandfather's work at the Viktor Frankl Institute of America.

It is my intention to incorporate logotherapeutic ideas and other psychological and Judaic messages in this volume, as that is what Rabbi Bulka stood for throughout his life.

Logotherapy, a term you will find often throughout this work, was originally developed by Viktor Frankl. It is, in short, therapy through

---

2. Ibid.

meaning. Understanding Frankl's perspective is crucial: meaning cannot and need not be created or manufactured. As articulated by Frankl's grandson, Alex Vesley, life itself offers an abundance of meaning, waiting for us to find, to recognize, or to discover. Unfortunately, in certain circumstances, it can also be lost or overlooked.

Contrary to popular belief, logotherapy is not solely intended for those in distress. As explained by Dr. Peggy Kleinplatz, a logotherapist and educator at the University of Ottawa, Viktor Frankl proposed three avenues to discover meaning: through one's contributions to the world, what they receive from it, and how they confront the unchangeable aspects of life. Frankl's counsel encourages us not to seek suffering but rather focus on finding purpose in our actions and experiences, allowing meaning to reveal itself organically.

Rabbi Bulka did suffer over his lifetime, and during times of difficulty and challenge, he managed to rise to the occasion. But he didn't wait to find meaning in times of hardship. He discovered it in the way he gave to the world, through his children, his vocation, his allocations, and everything he did in his spare time. The word "retire" was never in Rabbi Bulka's vocabulary, nor did he ever take a true "vacation" in his life. As you will see, he was deeply involved in everything he did, always with an eye towards meaning. Rabbi Bulka did not simply extol the benefits of logotherapy, but he exemplified and embodied them in everything that he did.

One of the focal points of my grandfather's extensive writings revolved around what is known as "Chapters of the Sages" or "*Pirkay Avot*" in Hebrew, which forms a crucial part of the *mishnaic* liturgy. Rabbi Bulka's deep appreciation for *Pirkay Avot* stemmed from its inherent richness in ethics, morality, and above all, meaningfulness. In fact, when I set out to learn with my grandfather in anticipation of becoming a *Bat Mitzvah* (coming of age for women in Judaism), he immediately chose to study *Pirkay Avot* with me, likely because of its meaningful messaging. He often remarked that logotherapy was, in essence, "applied Judaism 101." While Viktor Frankl did not explicitly make the connection between Judaism and logotherapy, my grandfather embraced many of the tenets of logotherapy as an inseparable part of Judaism, as evidenced by the teachings within *Pirkay Avot*. Thus, in the following chapters, I have endeavored to include relevant passages from *Pirkay Avot* to highlight the profound connection that my grandfather so clearly recognized. I have utilized my grandfather's own translation of *Pirkay Avot*, directly sourced from one of his many works on the subject, "*Pirkay Avos on Marriage*," with the generous permission granted by Ktav Publishing House. By incorporating these verses and teachings, I aim to illuminate the profound resonance between logotherapy and Judaism, through the lens and wisdom of *Pirkay Avot*.

Through learning about my grandfather's life, I realized how he recognized meaning everywhere and, in every way, including the way he injected humor and wit into his daily life. Frankl writes: "Humor was another of the soul's weapons in the fight for self-preservation. It is well known that humor, more than anything else in the human make-up, can afford an aloofness and an ability to rise above any situation, even if only for a few seconds."[3] Even in the face of a life-threatening illness, Rabbi Bulka's quick wit and "punny" sense of humor put those around him at ease.

When I set out to write this book, it was my own personal way of actualizing meaning during a difficult time, namely the cancer diagnosis that my grandfather had received. For me, the writing of this book has served as my own personal logotherapy during the challenging months that my grandfather faced a terminal illness, and the months following his death. But it also reminded me that it's possible to discover meaning in the mundane and always live with purpose and intention. My hope is that you, the reader, will not only learn more about Rabbi Bulka's life and the way he found meaning, but that you will be inspired and reinvigorated to live your own life more fully, and of course, meaningfully.

Rabbi Bulka often spoke about his desire to make the world a better place. In the pages that follow, I am confident that you will

3. Frankl, Viktor E., *Man's Search for Meaning*, (Boston, Massachusetts: Beacon Press, 2006), 43.

see his humble desire come to fruition, and that you will experience logotherapy in action. In one of his last interviews, Rabbi Buka said: "For me, the most important thing is for people to ask the question as early in life as they can: 'What can I do to make this world a better place?'" In the same interview, he said, "When you leave this world, in retrospect, you say to yourself, 'The world is a little better because I was here'"[4]. I can confidently say this was true about Rabbi Bulka; the world is undoubtedly a better place because he was in it.

Rabbi Bulka became known as "Canada's Rabbi" precisely because he filled his entire life and the lives of others with deep meaning and kindness. And of course, he earned this title after spending most of his adult years trying to create a better and kinder Canada.

I pray that this book can stand as testament to the extraordinary life he lived. Rabbi Bulka always believed that beyond the prayers we pray and the Torah we learn, there is always the necessity of being called to action. I hope that reading about Rabbi Bulka's extraordinary life serves as a call to action. I pray that it inspires the reader to look at Rabbi Bulka's life and realize that "I too can make a difference."

* * *

As I was writing this book, I tried to figure out the best way to capture my grandfather's essence. At the end of each chapter, I have included snippets from emails and letters my grandfather received after his diagnosis was made public and stories shared from family and friends across the world. These are a further testament to his success in leaving the world a better place than it was before.

I have also included the text of selected speeches or writings that Rabbi Bulka composed, because hearing his voice in this work will give the reader a truer understanding of Rabbi Bulka's greatness.

To understand the context of some of the messages that you will see scattered throughout the book, I will share the text of the letter that my grandfather, Rabbi Bulka, sent out to his congregation upon receiving his diagnosis:

---

4. CBC *Interview*, 2021.

Dear beloved Family Machzikei.

First and foremost, I trust that you and yours are well.

This past month has been, to say the least, quite eventful.

Just a few days ago, on Monday, January 4, I returned home from almost 4 weeks in the hospital.

I am overwhelmed with gratitude to you for your warm wishes that came in so many forms – prayer, calls, cards, e-mails, etc.

They are all so deeply appreciated. And so many people offered to help. I am grateful to everyone, deeply grateful.

Special thanks to dear Rabbi Scher and Shifra for their helpfulness at all times and to Reb Shimon and Esti Fogel for their immeasurable kindness during my hospital stay. In these pandemic days, there was very limited access to the hospital. Reb Shimon stepped in and came literally every day, in addition to doing so many other wonderful things. My gratitude is overflowing.

Now comes the hard part. During my stay, precipitated by fainting at home, the diligent crew at the Ottawa Hospital examined me quite thoroughly and started to uncover some serious issues.

Without getting into unnecessary detail, they found advanced cancer in the pancreas and liver. Needless to say, it came as a shock.

I have waited until now to share this with you as I wanted to do this only after meeting the oncology doctor to get the full picture. That meeting took place this past Thursday. I am writing to you all after Shabbat to share this with you if for no other reason than to head off wild speculation and also to be up front.

It is obvious that in these circumstances, some painful decisions have to be made.

In the face of what can be called an enormous struggle, I have decided to be with my dear family in New York.

They have set into motion the steps for appropriate medical intervention, starting with the remarkable crew at the Ottawa Hospital.

So, in the coming days the plan is to travel to New York.

This is *not* a goodbye letter. It is a thank you letter to you all for the wonderful years we shared together.

I hope to stay in touch and I hope that you will be in touch.

May you all be blessed with good health and vigour, and enjoy nahat from each other.

Having the privilege to serve as your Rabbi, and then as your Rabbi Emeritus, has been a great blessing, for which I am so grateful.

God bless you all.
Rabbi R. Bulka

# *Chapter 1*
# The Wake-Up Call

> "Truly, Ephraim is a dear son to Me, a child that is dandled! Whenever I have turned against him, My thoughts would dwell on him still. That is why My heart yearns for him; I will receive him back in love."
>
> – *Jeremiah 31:20*

It was a cold, winter November morning in Ottawa with snow on the ground as usual. Rabbi Bulka got ready to head to Congregation Machzikei Hadas on Virginia Drive, where he was the Rabbi. He was 32 years old, sprightly and passionate, and was straightening his tie before work when he encountered every parent's worst nightmare.

Rabbi Bulka did a routine check on his two-month-old son before leaving for work. The scene he encountered would be etched in his mind forever. His precious son, Ephraim Yechezkel, *z"l*[1], lay motionless in his crib.

He immediately began administering CPR, not realizing that his then seven-year-old son, Shmuel, was watching from afar. Meanwhile, Rabbi Bulka's eight-year-old daughter, Yocheved, and six-year-old daughter, Rena, were planning a two-month birthday celebration for Ephraim.

They were amid planning when they noticed their brother, Shmuel, sobbing at the top of the steps. "Was something wrong with our

---

1. *z"l* stands for the Hebrew words *Zichrono Livracha,* which is a term that means "He should be remembered in blessing".

birthday celebrations?" they wondered. Shmuel explained what he thought was happening.

Ambulances arrived, and screams of horror reverberated throughout the house as this nightmarish event unfolded.

The loss of Ephraim was devastating. People walked into my grandfather's home in hysterics. Shmuel recalls never having seen such a broken house in his life. When my grandfather was later asked about this tragic loss, he recalled his late wife, Naomi, *a"h*[2], suffering many miscarriages throughout the years before Ephraim was born.

> "She was a model of supreme dignity," Rabbi Bulka said about his late wife. "But nothing compares with having a baby that you hold in your hand. I remember it like it was yesterday. Every morning, we would check to see if the baby's okay, and the day Ephraim passed away, I looked in his room and saw something very wrong. He was lying motionless; he had died in his sleep. It was a shattering experience."

They later found out that Ephraim had passed away from SIDS, otherwise known as sudden infant death syndrome. Rabbi Bulka became involved in a SIDS organization with other bereaved parents, where there was opportunity to share stories and coping mechanisms. He desperately tried to figure out what could have gone wrong, as his son had been perfectly healthy. Rabbi Bulka considered this horrific tragedy "a game changer."

> "Until that point, everything was so good. I had a good job, happily married, nice kids. And this was all of a sudden a punch in the nose, that that's not the way life was always going to be... For me, the most important message was that it's in your hands to transmute what is a tragedy into something that can basically weigh down so heavily on you that you're immobilized for the rest of your life, or to say you now have the gift of life and you may not have realized how precious it was up until now, so now that you do, prove it."

---

2. *a"h* stands for the Hebrew words *Aleha HaShalom*, which is a term that means "May peace be upon him.

Not one to make empty statements, Rabbi Bulka did just that. "Death is a tragedy and there's no escaping it. But what you do after that happens is what defines it. "

That was the point in Rabbi Bulka's life when he decided to go beyond his job description as "Shul Rabbi" and do even more with his time.

It may very well be this moment in his life that led to his truly becoming the "Rabbi Bulka," "Canada's Rabbi," whom we love and miss today.

* * *

Many people face difficult life circumstances and plan to change at some point in the future. Rabbi Bulka is one of those few people who set out to change his life immediately.

Frankl, in his work on logotherapy, discusses one of the three major dimensions of human life: how we find meaning in the face of pain, suffering, and death. Frankl writes:

> The way in which a man accepts his fate and all the suffering it entails, the way in which he takes up his cross, gives him ample opportunity-even under the most difficult circumstances-to add a deeper meaning to his life. It may remain brave, dignified, and unselfish. Or in the bitter fight for self-preservation, he may forget his human dignity and become no more than an animal. Here lies the chance for a man either to make use of or forgo the opportunities of attaining the moral values that a difficult situation may afford him. And this decides whether he is worthy of his sufferings or not.[3]

In response to this tragedy that Rabbi Bulka endured, he chose to channel his suffering, a suffering which he admitted, more than forty years later, he was still enduring. He decided to write a book in memory of his dear son.

"When we are no longer able to change a situation – we are challenged to change ourselves".[4]

---

3. Frankl, *Man's Search for Meaning*, 62.
4. Ibid., 96

During this significant juncture in Rabbi Bulka's life, he confronted the profound truth embedded within the demand of *Pirkay Avot* to: "know from where you came, where you are going, and before Whom you will have to give account and reckoning."[5] Rabbi Bulka recognized the fleeting nature of life, understanding the importance of utilizing the time bestowed upon him to make a meaningful impact. He realized that the choices he made and the efforts he invested in his limited time would shape the narrative he would present when the time for evaluation arrived.

Embracing the wisdom encapsulated in *Pirkay Avot,* Rabbi Bulka internalized the imperative to live purposefully and conscientiously. He dedicated himself to diligent work and strived to make a positive difference, mindful of the ultimate responsibility to give an account for his actions and choices. His commitment to making the most of his allotted time exemplifies the essence of logotherapy, wherein individuals find meaning by recognizing their responsibility to utilize their time and abilities for the betterment of themselves and others. Rabbi Bulka's journey serves as a poignant reminder of the importance of seizing the present moment and actively engaging in a purposeful life, ensuring that when the time for reckoning arrives, one can proudly offer a compelling account of their endeavors.

## Chapter 1 – Letters

### LETTER #1

Dear Rabbi, it's interesting how you have touched so many people in so many different ways.

Even though I have always belonged to a different synagogue in Ottawa, my brother Martin Taller attended Machzeki Hadas... and then when his beautiful wife Gloria tragically passed away a number of years ago from cancer, I was asked to say the eulogy about her at her funeral.

After the service, Rabbi, you made a point to come up to me... to

5. Pirkay Avot 3:1, (Bulka, Ktav Publishing).

compliment me on the words I had just spoken saying "I have heard many eulogies in my life, but yours was one of the most beautiful meaningful and touching words I have ever heard."

Thank you, dear Rabbi…

I have never forgotten this because I have always had great respect for you. You're an amazing spiritual force, a vessel of Hashem placed here to guide us…and in your unique way, impart to us the blessings of Hashem.

Your comments have always held a special place in my heart.

### LETTER #2

Rabbi Bulka always seemed larger than life. Being involved in many of Ottawa Jewish community committees, I would always notice his presence spending valuable time attending several meetings on the same evening. Going above and beyond does not even begin to scratch the surface.

He would assess every situation and provide sage advice. I feel so fortunate to have witnessed how he assisted us in innumerable ways. His kindness is infectious and has made everyone better for knowing him.

On a more personal note, my whole family benefited from his kindness. He was a positive role model to all of us – Allan, Michal, Jonathan and myself. A case in point is when he drove to Montreal to visit my gravely ill mother in hospital and turned around and drove back to Ottawa. How one person could do so much and affect so many is incredulous.

### LETTER #3

The power of superlatives do not do justice to what Rabbi Bulka means to our family. Ironically, due to his humility, he has always been immune to accepting those same ego-boosting superlatives. But some things need to be said. We all know the Rabbi for the great leader, mentor, counsellor, teacher, scholar, and human that he is.

But please know this. For us, growing up in Ottawa in our home, he was more than this. By way of context, our grandmother (z"l) was born in Lithuania in around 1900, and arrived in Ottawa in 1948 after a 20 year detour in rural Brazil. She was a passionate Zionist who studied and trained in agriculture in Lithuania and longed to move to what-was-then Palestine. Circumstances waylaid those plans such that her and her extended family ended up moving to and farming in Manotick instead. In her home and at that time, the iconic and then-recently formed legacy of Theodore Hertzl was paramount.

Flash forward 30 years. In our mother's home in Ottawa that status of Dr. Theodore Herzl was replaced by Rabbi Dr. Reuven Bulka. With respect to our parents, there was no singular person other than their parents, who had more of a positive influence on how they thought, worshiped, lived their lives or raised their children.

Rabbi Bulka, we thank you for that, and everything you've done for us as a family over the last 50 years. Kol ha'kavod.

*Chapter 2*

# An Author is Born

"I can shake off everything as I write; my sorrows disappear, my courage is reborn."

– *Anne Frank*

To honor Ephraim's memory, Rabbi Bulka aptly chose to write a psychological commentary on *Pirkay Avot* (Wisdom of Our Fathers), fusing together his love of Judaism and psychology.

He painstakingly wrote a commentary on the first two chapters and sent it to several publishers. They showed little interest.

Feldheim Publishers responded by saying it was interesting, but they doubted he would be able to write the next four chapters. While Rabbi Bulka knew that there was a semblance of truth to the publisher's comment, he felt that it offered him an avenue. If he could carry it through, then he would have a book. The challenge was gripping, and Rabbi Bulka worked feverishly to complete the volume.

The goal of the book was to write a psychological commentary that connected one *mishnah* (portion) to the next, as he was certain there was meaning behind the juxtaposition of the *mishnayot* (portions).

Nothing in Rabbi Bulka's world was "impossible," and the publication of this important work proved that. Rabbi Bulka had been turned down numerous times from numerous publishers, all telling him that the idea would never come to fruition. It is likely in part because of their doubt that he persevered to prove that it was not impossible.

Eventually, the book was published as a concrete memorial for

Rabbi Bulka's son, Ephraim. The book was entitled *As a Tree by the Waters,* although my grandfather admitted that the abstract title didn't quite elucidate the subject of the book.

For the next book that Rabbi Bulka wrote, he did not make the same mistake. It was titled *The Haggadah Connection*; it was a *sefer* (Jewish book) on *Haggadah Shel Pesach,* a companion work to be used during the *seder* on Passover.

My grandfather shared with me his discomfort about sharing an endless amount of unconnected *vorts* (ideas) regarding Pesach. He believed that it was more important to discover the purpose of the *seder.* After much probing, it became clear to Rabbi Bulka that the goal was to reconnect us to our spiritual roots by recalling our history, discussing the beauty of our faith, and our appreciation of how we got to this place. Rabbi Bulka illustrated this clearly in what became a bestselling work.

From then on, Rabbi Bulka rarely put his pen down, as his ideas flowed freely until he had written nearly forty books, on a variety of topics, emerging in all shapes and sizes.

One of the first books Rabbi Bulka wrote was inspired by a book called *Wit and Wisdom of Mark Twain.* When he flipped through the book of elucidated quotations, Rabbi Bulka wondered how he could adapt the concept for the Talmud.

Rabbi Bulka immediately reached out to a representative from the Peter Pauper Press and suggested his idea: "Wit and Wisdom of the Talmud." Within one month, Rabbi Bulka sent in his final copy, and it was published soon after. In fact, he even wrote a sequel. Rabbi Bulka shared that he did not consider these publications to be books in the traditional sense.

Personally, I am inspired by Rabbi Bulka's alacrity. Rabbi Bulka was a dreamer, but perhaps more importantly, he was a doer. Rabbi Bulka was committed to bringing his ideas to fruition. He didn't let lightbulb moments dissolve into the abyss. Instead, he got to work immediately, and had the rare opportunity to see his ideas in print, literally.

In a discussion about discovering one's own potential, Frankl quotes Goethe in *The Doctor and the Soul:* "How can we learn to know ourselves? Never by reflection, but by action. Try to do your duty and you will soon find out what you are. But what is your duty? The demands of each day."[1]

This sentiment is echoed almost perfectly in *Pirkay Avot* where it is written: "Study is not most important, rather doing".[2] In other words, logotherapy, like *Pirkay Avot*, emphasizes the importance of action.

The first lesson from Rabbi Bulka in making the world a better place and discovering a life of meaning? Don't just dream. Do.

Instead of fumbling through life, wondering and contemplating how to live up to your potential, logotherapy would suggest engaging in the "demands of each day" that speak to your soul. Through action, you will actualize your potential, and in doing so, discover a more meaningful life, and like Rabbi Bulka, hopefully, a more meaningful world.

* * *

It is worth circling back to the true beginning of Rabbi Bulka's writing career: his dissertation. In the late 1960s, Rabbi Bulka was the Rabbi of Machizkei Hadas but initially found that he had a lot more time than he'd expected. He chose to return to school, the University of Ottawa, to earn his doctorate in psychology.

He conducted his thesis on logotherapy and the Talmud.

The dissertation committee consisted of a panel of five people: the thesis supervisor, two internal committee members, and two external examiners. When Rabbi Bulka first presented his thesis, the internal sponsors thought it was great, but the two outsiders dissented. The rule was that one could not have two objectors to a thesis. The deadline loomed, and my grandfather looked at his options.

Option A was to appeal to the senate of the university, but that was unlikely to prove successful, because it would not likely overrule the examiner's objections. Option B was to switch courses and write an entirely new thesis. My grandfather would only have ten days to do this, but he chose Option B and persevered.

---

1. Frankl, Viktor E., *The Doctor and The Soul: From Psychotherapy to Logotherapy*. Second Vintage Books ed, (New York, NY: Random House, Inc., 1986), 56.
2. Pirkay Avot 1:17, (Bulka, Ktav Publishing).

Rabbi Bulka recalls sleeping about an hour or two per night during that ten-day period (Knowing my grandfather, I doubt this was the last time he ran on so little sleep-with all that he accomplished, one wonders how he had time to sleep at all). Instead of a paper on logotherapy and the Talmud, he wrote a paper on a comparison of logotherapy and other religious denominations, including but not limited to Judaism. He wrote a 145-page thesis in ten days, submitted it, and it was accepted miraculously.

The positive outcome of this ordeal was that my grandfather was able to parcel his thesis into several books and articles. "It was tense for a bit," Rabbi Bulka recalled, "but worked out well upon looking back."

In one of the many works Rabbi Bulka wrote on logotherapy, a book entitled *Work, Love, Suffering, Death: A Jewish/Psychological Perspective through Logotherapy*, I came across a quote that Rabbi Bulka referenced at the age of 53, a quote that he continued to live by:

> The more a man is interested in merely keeping himself alive the more he cuts himself off from meaningful living. In the pursuit of years, he wastes the days. The more man realizes he is mortal, destined to die, the more he will try to accomplish, thus perhaps even gaining immortality.[3]

When I quoted this to Rabbi Bulka in the face of his own life-threatening illness and asked him if his perspective had changed, he expressed just the opposite. "It has been strengthened," he said. "When I wrote that, I knew no one lived forever, I wasn't living with any illusions. I encountered it in the Rabbinate on an almost daily basis."

Throughout Rabbi Bulka's illness, he lived by this mantra. In deciding on his cancer treatment plan, Rabbi Bulka prioritized quality of life. He preferred to have a clear head during his last few months, rather than endure the poisonous side effects of the most aggressive chemotherapy.

* * *

3. Bulka, Reuven P., *Work, Love, Suffering & Death: A Jewish/psychological Perspective Through Logotherapy*, (Lanham, Maryland: J. Aronson, 1997), 114.

Rabbi Bulka did not tell a soul outside of his family and the university staff that he was pursuing his doctorate. He did not want anyone in his congregation to feel that he was too busy to be approached-he wanted to ensure he was just as available and present as always. One day, he announced he had his Ph.D., much to the shul's shock, as no one would have ever suspected based on the amount of attention Rabbi Bulka had continued to give.

Another Rabbi Bulka lesson: Work hard, but don't let it interfere with your ability to give each person you encounter your undivided attention. And practice what you preach.

## Chapter 2 – Letters

### LETTER #1

Sunday night with Rabbi Bulka, 580 CFRA Ottawa Radio. July 20, 2014

We contacted Rabbi Bulka when we moved to Ottawa in 2011. We knew about him since we had one of his books, "The Quest for Ultimate Meaning: Principles and Applications of Logotherapy" (1979) with a foreword by Viktor E Frankl. He completed his master's thesis (1969) and his Doctoral Dissertation (1971) at the University of Ottawa on the topic of Viktor E. Frankl's logotherapy. Viktor Frankl was a psychiatrist from Vienna who was also a survivor of the Holocaust. His most famous book is "Man's Search for Meaning." Rabbi Bulka often spoke about how he met Frankl for the first time before Frankl offered a presentation at the University of Ottawa in 1968. We knew that when we were in the presence of Rabbi Bulka, we were in the presence of someone who was an internationally respected scholar of meaning-centered counseling. It was a humbling and fantastic experience to be invited to his radio show as guests. We were being interviewed about our work at the Ottawa Institute of Logotherapy, although we felt as if we could have turned the table around and asked him all the questions we had! It was a one-of-a kind, unique, and unrepeatable honor to be with him in the studio. His words will not be forgotten, and his example remains.

## LETTER #2

One can only be grateful to God for presenting a gift of a Rabbi Reuven Pinhas ben Yehudit, may you be blessed, for those blessed, to be in your midst or periphery.

What you have done and do each day through sermons recalled, teachings remembered, books written by you, now, embedded in our daily acts by having motivated us, your readers, to be better human beings, more spiritually encompassed, continually, recognizing one cannot lead a recess or coffee break existence, but, that life is a continuum of Machshava, dibbur and ma'assei, good thoughts, words and deeds. You, dear Rabbi Bulka, are an exemplar for us, of all of those and so much more.

Your commentary on "The Ethics of the Fathers" is a magnum opus, a *GPS* for moral clarity, giving life meaning to generations, who now study it, from grandfather to child to grandchild. Your commentary on the Shmoneh Esre, written in partnership with your grandchild, is a guide to understanding the meaning of thanksgiving and blessing of God; and, how to plead before the Holy One, for our needs, as individuals, a community, a people, a land and the world, with humility, yet God given dignity, by walking in God's holy ways.

Dear Rabbi Bulka, I thank God and your parents for having created you, as a treasured gift on our life journeys, making our life much more meaningful, by giving us greater meaning. This you did, so remarkably, in the movie with Richard Dreyfus on Frankl's Choice. "Man's Search for Meaning" is certainly found in you; and you give it to everyone, gifted with your presence, teaching and books.

My family and I thank God for your presence in our lives, giving us a gift of thus, teaching and sharing with others, in the model of your kindness, and example of your nobility of character and aristocracy of your soul.

*Chapter 3*

# Not Such Canadian Roots

"The taller a tree, the deeper its roots."

– *Matshona Dhliwayo*

To truly understand Rabbi Bulka's extraordinary life, we must explore his roots. Rabbi Bulka was born in England on D-Day, June 6, 1944. His memories of England are non-existent, as his family moved to Providence, Rhode Island when he was only two. Rabbi Bulka's father, Rabbi Yaakov Bulka, was a rebbe there, and eventually moved from Providence to New York to be a Rebbe in Talmud Torah.

After several years of living in New York, a Rabbinic position became available in the Bronx. The shul was called Khal Adath Yeshurun, and many prestigious Rabbis had previously served there. Rabbi Yaakov Bulka was encouraged to apply for the job, but as my grandfather recalled, "It was a total longshot. He had no experience as a pulpit Rabbi, and no real training."

Miraculously, he made it through the first round. Much to the family's surprise, he was chosen as Rabbi after the second cut. My grandfather remembers the ecstasy and excitement reverberating throughout the house. It was more than just a job. Rabbi Yaakov Bulka was immensely talented, but had spent his career until then hopping from one teaching job to another. He was used to living a life of uncertainty; and this job finally provided a certain measure of calm and predictability.

The people responsible for selecting Rabbi Yaakov Bulka saw his outstanding qualities, and in turn, he justified their confidence and became one of the most revered Rabbis of his time. It wasn't instantaneous, as he was a rookie in the congregational world. He dedicated himself fully to his shul and congregation. He had never received formal training for the pulpit, but his appreciation of humankind and ability to commiserate, counsel, and inspire others made him a true gem in the Rabbinic world.

My grandfather recalled his father giving intricate *Divrei Torah* (Words of Torah). So intricate, in fact, that when they once tried to unravel some of the speeches to put them in print, they were impossible to reproduce. He spoke eloquently, with passion, strong dedication, and commitment. He ended each speech with the words "*Uva LeTzion Goel Venomar Amen,*" Let the redeemer come to Zion.

As Rabbi Yaakov Bulka's reputation grew, his congregation began to blossom. Any time there was a *simcha* (celebration) in the congregation, Rebbetzin Yehudis Bulka, Rabbi Yaakov Bulka's wife, put together a gift package for the *ba'ale simcha* (the hosts of the occasion). It is worth noting that the annual salary for a pulpit Rabbi at this time, albeit in the year 1949, was not more than $5,000; but the gifts came straight from my great-grandparents' pockets because those were the kind of people they were.

I asked Rabbi Bulka what it was like being the son of the Rabbi. He told me that it came with great advantages, as most people wanted to be on good terms with the Rabbi. It did have its downsides, though. Rabbi Bulka recalled his nine-year-old self in the downstairs bathroom of the shul, taking out a cigarette and getting ready to smoke.

Someone walked in the bathroom and caught him. Rabbi Bulka recalls "shivering in his boots." The congregant who caught him told Rabbi Bulka that he wouldn't tell his parents if he promised never to try a cigarette again. Rabbi Bulka complied and remarked later, "I never broke my promise."

All things considered, Rabbi Bulka's childhood as the son of a Rabbi was pleasant. My grandfather recalled a few elements that stood out to him from his childhood. The first was the obvious love that existed between his parents and the congregation. As my grandfather explained to me, the original shul was in a neighborhood in the East Bronx, an area becoming less safe with each passing day.

At that time, Rabbis often resorted to selling their shul and pocketing the money. Rabbi Yaakov Bulka could have done this, but he wanted to rebuild the shul in another place for the sake of his beloved congregation. He found another location, but the journey to building the shul was not easy, as there was no wealthy person in the community to call on to fund the project. Rabbi Yaakov Bulka set out to do the fundraising on his own.

When they began setting up the new shul, my great-grandfather was extremely scrupulous and honest, a trait that my grandfather inherited. The new shul's location presented some neighborhood competition between shuls, and my great-grandfather refused to ask anyone holding another shul membership to join his congregation.

Rabbi Bulka recalled his father running back and forth between two shuls: the established one, and the one he was building in a new neighborhood in hopes of its being a safer place to congregate. Rabbi Yaakov Bulka was committed to running prayer services in both synagogues, but my grandfather explained that this extreme dedication came at a great sacrifice.

When Rabbi Bulka was just sixteen years old, his father, Rabbi Yaakov Bulka, suffered a major heart attack. He was ordered on bed rest for 6 months, which was the typical treatment plan at the time.

The shul could not afford to hire another Rabbi, and so my grandfather was drafted into service. He recalls the congregation being very understanding and forgiving. "That was how I got my on-the-job Rabbinic training." Rabbi Bulka, at the age of 16, began leading services and giving sermons. Though he didn't perform weddings and funerals, all other Rabbinic responsibilities were left under his jurisdiction until his father became healthy enough to resume the pulpit.

Even after Rabbi Yaakov Bulka returned in full health, my grandfather spent time leading services in the old synagogue so that his father could dedicate his time to building the new one.

Rabbi Bulka recalled that he originally wanted to be a doctor or lawyer; but once he became immersed in Rabbinic work, he never thought twice about his own career goals. The Rabbinate, in his words, is a wonderful opportunity to affect people's lives. "It was too good to be true."

My grandfather also recalled his younger years as a student, telling me that he wasn't always such a star. He recalled having a crisis where he had failed math class, and his parents were so angry at him because they were insistent that he could do better. My grandfather pushed himself and received a 96% so as not to disappoint his parents. In fact, he graduated as valedictorian in elementary school, and later as valedictorian for Yiddish during his *Smichah* (Rabbinical ordination) ceremony.

* * *

A person often finds his or her calling in life through unexpected channels. But, as Rabbi Bulka has shown us, rising to the challenges that life inevitably brings will certainly yield more opportunities for growth and self-discovery. Rabbi Bulka did not originally have any plans to become a Rabbi, as he observed the intense demands of his father's time. He could easily have let the few months he spent as interim Rabbi dry up in a vacuum. Instead, Rabbi Bulka welcomed this crisis as an opportunity, allowing this journey to provide him direction for the future. As the ancient wisdom of *Pirkay Avot* reminds us, "The day is short, the task is great."[1] In essence, life is filled with countless tasks, but it would be futile to spend our limited time solely pursuing them. Sometimes, the task at hand is right before us, waiting to be acknowledged.

Rabbi Bulka serves as a shining example of this ancient message, which is demonstrated further by through logotherapy. As noted above, the way to come to know ourselves, according to Frankl, is through action. It is worth quoting again: "Try to do your duty and you will soon find out what you are. But what is your duty? The demands of each day".[2]

I don't think anyone can imagine a world where Rabbi Bulka

1. Pirkay Avot 2:15, (Bulka, Ktav Publishing).
2. Frankl, *Doctor and the Soul*, 56.

was not a Rabbi. Rabbi Bulka demonstrated that embracing life challenges can open the door to personal growth and self-discovery. I encourage the reader to reflect and inquire: What valuable insights has my personal journey unveiled, guiding me towards the path I should pursue?

*Chapter 4*

# Gift of Life

> "Looking back over the many years that I have been involved in healthcare, I recall hearing many complaints and I have no doubts that we humans are far from perfect. But as a spy on the other side, who gained entry in difficult circumstances, I hope my observations that we are so fortunate to have such a wonderful system with so many caring people will be the theme that you bear in mind when you think about our healthcare system. We are blessed. We are fortunate. We are lucky. And therefore, should be very grateful."
>
> – *Rabbi Bulka*

Perhaps among his greatest accomplishments is Rabbi Bulka's pioneering and championing the idea of organ donation in Orthodox Judaism. He is one of the few responsible for Orthodox Canadians, and Orthodox Jews in general, becoming organ donors.

Rabbi Bulka originally became involved in 1991. He received a call asking if he would be interested in starting a kidney donor Foundation. He was later asked to join a provincial committee on organ donation, which eventually morphed into the "Trillium Gift of Life Network" and with Rabbi Bulka's involvement, became national. He was originally slated to serve a three year term as the chair, but he instead ended up serving in that role for eleven years.

It was extremely important to Rabbi Bulka that somebody Jewish be at the forefront of saving lives, not just as the recipients.

The organization really took off when Ronnie Gavsie took over as President and CEO. Upon speaking to Gavsie about my grandfather's involvement in the organization, she said:

> "I was responsible for organ donation and transplants. Stats came out sent to me and other members of the team every day that would tell you how many lives have been saved since the day before- or that year compared to the year before. Your grandfather received it and was also so motivating. Whenever he saw the numbers going down, I'd hear from him in the sweetest, nicest way, 'Have you turned over every rock to make sure our system is working well?'"

Gavsie recalls Rabbi Bulka guiding her through every major decision as CEO. All of his policy decisions came down to one single question: Will it save more lives, or won't it?

One of the highlights of the organization was a donor recognition ceremony. Donors who had lost family members attended and were presented with a picture of their loved one. They were handed a gold medal with their loved one's name on it. At each ceremony, Rabbi Bulka delivered the keynote address. It was an event he never missed.

Everyone at Trillium Gift of Life looked forward to Rabbi Bulka's speech each year. Gavsie recalls:

> "He would take us on a journey and we never knew how it would have anything to do with organ donation until the end. He might start with a sports figure in the news, but he'd always find a way to connect it. He spoke with humor, brilliance, and warmth. And never did he bring a note."

Michael Ward, Family Services Advisor at Trillium Gift of Life, added that Rabbi Bulka's speeches were always current; and he was always able to discern when levity was needed, or when it might be a good time to add in a signature Rabbi Bulka pun.

Michael Ward and Rabbi Bulka traveled across the province roughly six to seven times a year to honor and personally shake the hand of every donor. Ward recalls speaking to the donor families following their visits across Ontario, all noting that speaking to Rabbi Bulka was a highlight.

When Rabbi Bulka would visit Trillium headquarters, he always made the rounds to say hello to each member of the team, regardless of his or her role. Rabbi Bulka had special kosher meals brought in during his visits; and Ward humorously notes that he often finished half of Rabbi Bulka's meals, as Rabbi Bulka was already on to the next task at hand and didn't often make the time to finish lunch.

Rabbi Bulka was always known to be positive, warm, and kind, but he also had a keen sense of how to manage workplace politics. He was able to navigate controversy and conflict in a way that everyone felt they had won. As an aside, when Rabbi Bulka was interviewed following his diagnosis and asked how he felt about the outpouring of love, he humorously regretted that he hadn't entered the field of politics.

After Rabbi Bulka had received the Order of Canada (see Chapter 18), the first time he was back at Trillium, the staff ordered a huge cake for him. They ushered him into the boardroom for a "meeting" and he was met with "Hoorays," "Congrats," and "Surprise!" At that meeting, Rabbi Bulka exclaimed to the staff that the three most important things in his life were "my family, my congregation, and the Trillium Gift of Life Network."

It is worth noting that my grandfather himself always carried a card rendering himself an organ donor and encouraged others to do so as well.

He did whatever he could to save lives in ways that were accessible to him. He personifies the maxim from *Pirkay Avot* "It is not up to you to complete the task, but you are not free to desist from it."[1] Rabbi Bulka recognized that he couldn't single-handedly save every individual in need of an organ. However, he wholeheartedly dedicated himself to utilizing his capabilities and made a significant impact.

* * *

1. Pirkay Avot 2:16, (Bulka, Ktav Publishing).

Though fortuitous, Rabbi Bulka's involvement with cancer treatments began years before his own diagnosis. Rabbi Bulka's first wife, Naomi Bulka, *a"h,* passed away from cancer at the young age of 55, leaving behind a husband, five children, and many grandchildren. Because of his personal understanding of the havoc that cancer can wreak, Rabbi Bulka became involved in the Ottawa Regional Cancer foundation.

According to the tribute that the cancer center wrote following my grandfather's death,

> Rabbi Bulka contributed to some of the Ottawa Regional Cancer Foundation's most important memories and milestones. Among other leadership roles, he served on our Board of Directors, co-chaired and played key roles in major fundraising campaigns, was a member of the President's Advisory Council, and never missed an opportunity to contribute with a smile and kind word.
>
> Rabbi Bulka was an exceptional collaborator who excelled at bringing people together. He was instrumental in helping the Foundation build partnerships across the cancer-care community, including with The Ottawa Hospital, Queensway Carleton Hospital, Élisabeth Bruyère Hospital, and the Canadian Cancer Society. In Rabbi Bulka's words: "We're all better when we work together." Across Eastern Ontario, his influence and collaborative spirit truly transformed local cancer care.
>
> Rabbi Bulka was humble and gracious, particularly in applauding the contributions of others. He enjoyed presenting Kindness Awards to staff at the Foundation and The Ottawa Hospital Research Institute, among others, and always shared words of gratitude when invited to bestow the Carole and Norman Zagerman Compassionate Care Award. We were an honoured beneficiary of his personal generosity as well; proceeds from two of his books were gifted to the Foundation for aid in cancer research.
>
> Rabbi Bulka's legacy and presence at the Foundation and Maplesoft-Jones Centre for Cancer Survivorship will be felt for years to come. Understanding the important role that faith and spirituality can play for families facing cancer, he was instrumen-

tal in creating the Centre's Multi-Faith and Meditation Suite. Our Rabbi Bulka Family Room was named in his honour by proud community donors Barbara Crook and Dan Greenberg, and our Rabbi Bulka Award recognizes exemplary service in the community to those facing cancer. It is the highest honour the Foundation can bestow.[2]

The foundation's CEO and founder Michael Maidment stated: "He was not just a friend, he was family, and he made Ottawa a better place to live for us all."

* * *

In addition to his involvement with cancer patients and treatments, Rabbi Bulka was also the first Vice Chair of Pallium Canada, an organization dedicated to providing palliative care for individuals and families. Palliative care, according to CEO Jeff Moat, is a part of healthcare that does not get the attention it deserves. Rabbi Bulka was a committed and active member of the board and a true pioneer and contributor to palliative care for patients in need.

Rabbi Bulka spent the last few months of his own life in palliative care, giving his family a firsthand understanding of the field's importance. Rabbi Bulka, of course, was one step ahead of the rest of us, putting emphasis on this much overlooked part of healthcare long before it would affect him in a personal way.

His involvement in the healthcare field as a volunteer knew no bounds. Rabbi Bulka expressed that if he hadn't become a Rabbi, he probably would have gone to medical school. Clearly, Rabbi Bulka was able to use his affinity towards medicine to help him in the Rabbinate. Whenever he was able to, he endeavored to save lives.

* * *

Rabbi Bulka recalled listening to the news one afternoon when an interruption was made declaring that the local blood bank was running

2. "In Memory of Rabbi Bulka," Ottawa Regional Cancer Foundation, accessed July, 10 2023, https://www.ottawacancer.ca/in-memory-of-Rabbi-bulka/.

low on blood. They requested that anyone eligible should come and donate. Rabbi Bulka was about 15 minutes away from the donation site and didn't think twice before re-routing to 85 Plymouth Street to donate blood.

"I was hooked," Rabbi Bulka explained. A rare thing for someone to say about donating blood. But Rabbi Bulka quickly calculated how many times a year he was eligible to give, and he went on to become a regular blood donor. When he hit about one hundred and fifteen blood donations, he got the idea that he wanted to donate blood 1000 times. He realized, though, that at the rate he was eligible to give, that would prove impossible.

Rabbi Bulka, once again not deterred by the word "impossible," searched for other ways of giving blood that allowed a person to give more often. He found a way to donate every two weeks, or 24 times a year. Eventually, he found out he could donate platelets once a week.

His blood donations had reached around 300 when he unfortunately had to stop donating due to blood pressure issues. Rabbi Bulka joked that he was so excited about giving blood that his blood pressure would go up, and he would be turned down!

"It takes a little bit of time," Rabbi Bulka explained, "but it's very useful. It helps people and saves lives, and I was happy to do it. It all started with an emergency call on the radio. Moral of the story: always listen to the radio."

I'd like to add another "moral." Always listen out for ways to help. And then help. Rabbi Bulka didn't waste a moment thinking about whether he wanted to heed the call of the blood bank. His compass was always pointed in the direction of helping others, and as such, he didn't have to think twice about changing his plans and going to donate.

Dear reader: take this opportunity to re-adjust your moral compass, ensuring that you are always willing, eager, and ready to help when there is a need.

Logotherapy says that the first of the three ways to find meaning in life is through what you give to the world. From this chapter alone, it is clear that Rabbi Bulka used each moment of his life to give to the world, in whatever way he could.

Frankl writes:

> It did not really matter what we expected from life, but rather what life expected from us. We needed to stop asking about the meaning of life, and instead to think of ourselves as those who were being questioned by life – daily and hourly. Our answer must consist, not in talk and meditation, but in right action and in right conduct. Life ultimately means taking the responsibility to find the right answer to its problems and to fulfill the tasks which it constantly sets for each individual.[3]

Rabbi Bulka clearly lived these words. Though he was quite a philosophical man, having dedicated years to pursuing a doctorate, teaching, and extolling the system of logotherapy, Rabbi Bulka understood that he had to act "in right action and in right conduct".[4] Rabbi Bulka spent the time solving problems that he found in the world and fulfilling his own personal duty to solve those problems.

## Chapter 4 – Letters

### LETTER #1

Rabbi Bulka cares about the community and helping people. I met him during a Gift of Life Celebration at his synagogue. I presented twice, once while I was waiting for a lifesaving kidney transplant and then once again a couple of years later when I was asked to speak after I received my transplant.

You can tell he cared about people.

### LETTER #2

We met Rabbi Bulka a few times at events honouring Organ Donors and Recipients. My husband and I stuck out like sore thumbs wheeling our

3. Frankl, *Man's Search for Meaning*, 70.
4. Ibid., 69.

second child through the synagogue to honour our first child who died from a head trauma when he was 16 months. A few of his organs were successfully harvested, but we never had any feedback from the Trillium Foundation or the families. Rabbi Bulka went out of his way to thank us and make us feel special whenever we attended these events. His empathy and kindness forever left its mark. We cherish those moments along with the happy memories our son gave to us in his short life.

### LETTER #3

I worked many years ago with Rabbi Bulka (RB) on the Organ Donation Committee through the Kidney Foundation. My father, Ben Franklin (former Mayor of Nepean), died of heart disease and I wanted to raise awareness of the importance of organ donation as a tribute to his memory. This was my first welcome exposure to RB's tireless energy, drive, and enthusiasm to raise social consciousness and to make the world a better place. Later encounters with RB centered around my work as a trauma therapist and grief counselor when RB interviewed me on his radio show in 2018. I loved our on-air dialogue and his wise observations about the nature and expression of grief, as well as the importance of serving others as a means of personal recovery. We made good co-hosts that night! What touched me the most, however, was when RB called me the next day to make sure I had gotten home safe and sound as the broadcast aired late at night. This was so kind and chivalrous! I was touched by this marvelous man's gentlemanly quality. I see it echoed in my partner in life, Patrick McGarry (another huge fan of RB!). Rabbi Bulka -your kindness, love of life and dedication to the service of others has moved and inspired us to no end. We are so grateful to know you and send our love. Shalom chaver. XO

### LETTER #4

Upon hearing and learning of what we have been doing at the Ottawa Integrative Cancer Centre (*OICC*), its foundation and subsequently the Centre for Health Innovation, Rabbi Bulka became a supporter and advocate for this vision of integrative and holistic care. Having been hosted with my wife Sarah on Rabbi Bulka's radio show on numerous occasions and having his support at many events has been an incredible gift to us and me very personally. Rabbi Bulka, the kindness and breadth you offer in your embrace is extraordinary. I am deeply grateful for who you are, what you stand for, and the warmth of your encouragement and leadership.

## LETTER #5

Maya Angelou famously said that people will forget what you said or did but never forget how you made them feel. For the children, youth and families we serve and all of our staff alike – Rabbi Bulka makes us feel only love. His presence, gentle demeanor and helpful hands have served The Children's Hospital of Eastern Ontario with boundless compassion, energy and heart.

I was trying to find a way to best describe Rabbi Bulka's contribution to *CHEO* over the years. He was an honorary board member for the past twenty years, so he's a volunteer. He's been generously donating time and fundraising for us since 1989 – in fact, his smile lights up every *CHEO* Telethon set as he sets out to maximize all "Miracle Matches." He's a generous donor.

He's lit the menorah in our main lobby most Hanukkahs and counsels Jewish families whenever they need it throughout the year. He's a beloved spiritual advisor. Rabbi Bulka played an instrumental role in helping to renovate and relaunch our Spiritual and Quiet Room. He's a builder.

Rabbi Bulka brings community together unlike anyone else can to enhance the patient experience onsite. He is a visionary. He has invited me and many *CHEO* physicians and researchers to participate on his radio show. He's an excellent storyteller.

As it turns out, it's near impossible to succinctly describe everything Rabbi Bulka has done as his impact has so many layers and each contribution means so much. He is love. And we love him back.

## RABBI BULKA, OP-ED, OTTAWA CITIZEN, JANUARY 13, 2021[5]

Of all the op-ed pieces I have written in my life, this one is, aside from being the most recent, also the most unique.

It is written from my hospital bed in the General campus of The Ottawa Hospital following a few weeks of wrestling with major health challenges. It is also written in the unique capacity as a self-appointed health care "spy." No one hired me, but I felt compelled to share with you the results of my espionage.

I have been fortunate enough to be involved in the health-care system for many years, and like all of you, have heard and read some fierce criticisms of the health-care system. No system created by humans can be perfect and health care is no exception. I both recognize and am in no way dismissive of the enormous challenges we face in sustaining and strengthening health-care delivery in Canada. But being on the other side and watching the goings-on with no one being aware of my doing so, has offered me a perspective it would be irresponsible not to share.

Sometimes we actually find it difficult to say nice things. But I have great difficulty finding anything not nice to say about the system as I have experienced it from the other side. Without any exaggeration, I can affirm that no one in the entire array of health-care providers has been anything less than excellent, sensitive and supportive. I am referring to the medical team – the physicians, nurses and therapists. But it extends equally to the attendants, the cleaners, indeed the entire staff who cheerfully brings me my meals and attends to cleaning the rooms, contributing to the management of such a complex operation.

All of them play a vital role in my care – and the care of all the other patients receiving treatment at The Ottawa Hospital. Without exception, they have demonstrated the deepest sense of commitment. Their dedication is beyond incredible. Their selflessness and devotion are beyond reproach.

These are not just my impressions. This is the evidence I have collected regarding my own experience and that which I have observed in

5. Bulka, Rabbi Reuven. "Op-ed," *Ottawa Citizen*, January 13, 2021.

my self-appointed capacity as a spy. Everyone in this system cares, and everyone in this system demonstrates devotion to a shared mission. Everyone is understanding. Everyone is kind. If I were to look with a powerful microscope, I would be hard-pressed to find a flaw in the delivery of healthcare. To be sure, as I noted above, no system is perfect, but we are pretty close and have so very much to be proud of in the way health care is provided in our community.

It is always easy to complain and undoubtedly there are things that could and should be better. But those deficiencies must not blur our vision regarding the big, wonderful embracing reality that the health care system actually is what it claims to be: a system that cares about our health. And passionately so.

Looking back over the many years that I have been involved in health care, I recall hearing many complaints and I have no doubts that we humans are far from perfect. But as a spy on the other side, who gained entry in difficult circumstances, I hope my observations that we are so fortunate to have such a wonderful system with so many caring people will be the theme that you bear in mind when you think about our health-care system. We are blessed. We are fortunate. We are lucky. And therefore, should be very grateful.

I know that I am.

Rabbi Dr. Reuven Bulka

*Chapter 5*

# We Love our Troops

> "We love our troops because of their selflessness.
>
> We love our troops because of their unswerving love of Canada.
>
> We love our troops because of their bravery and dignity in combat
>
> and
>
> We love our troops because through them, we gain a more vivid, vital appreciation of all the veterans who fought, on behalf of Canada, for global freedom."
>
> – *Rabbi Bulka, Remembrance Day 2007*

Perhaps one of the most meaningful moments after my grandfather's diagnosis was a ceremony for which I was personally present. It was a freezing January day in New York, with snow starting to fall (making it truly feel like Canada), and each of Rabbi Bulka's five children, masked and distanced (at the height of the Covid-19 pandemic), stood in my parents' backyard with whichever of their children happened to be local.

From an outsider's perspective, the scene was amusing. There was a large Canadian flag in the backyard and men in uniform casually walking down the block. I recall a neighbor texting my husband asking him what was going on.

It was surreal. We all stood there, freezing, but with warmth in our hearts as we watched our grandfather and father receive a Medallion for Distinguished Service from the Canadian military, presented by Brigadier General Keith Osmond, Deputy Military Advisor Major

Rick Cameron, and the Honorable Bob Rae, former Premier of Ontario, and current Canadian Ambassador to the United Nations.

Not only was it special to be part of the ceremony, but it was incredibly humbling to see in action what my grandfather had meant to Canada. The present work has taken so many interviews to even get a taste of what Rabbi Bulka did for his community. This was one of the first opportunities I had to witness the awesomeness of his public life firsthand.

You may be wondering what my grandfather did to deserve such an honor.

To understand, we'd have to travel back to November 11, 1991.

My grandfather was the Rabbi at Machzikei Hadas at the time; but his involvement with the city and country expanded greatly when Rabbi Bulka received a call from the Dominion Command of the Royal Canadian Legion. This organization oversaw the annual ceremony to be conducted at the National War Memorial on November 11. The annual ceremony holds great significance for Canadians as it is broadcasted live on all the country's TV stations, turning it into a momentous occasion for the entire nation. Until this point, another Rabbi had addressed the large crowd each year. When he announced his retirement, Rabbi Bulka, the only Rabbi in the city who was also a citizen of Canada, was asked to take his place.

It is worth noting that November 11, a day that became auspicious in coining the term "Canada's Rabbi," was the same day, many years earlier, that Rabbi Bulka's son, Ephraim, had been taken from the world.

For anyone who knew Rabbi Bulka, there were probably two things that stood out about him, especially at an outdoor speaking event. One, regardless of the temperature, he did not wear a coat. Rabbi Bulka claimed that he was simply "not cold." Even at the Remembrance Day ceremonies in the frigid Canadian November weather, he never wore any sort of topcoat, only his classic blue suit and perhaps a sweater underneath if it were truly below freezing. He once remarked that it would be insulting to the soldiers at war to wear a coat when they weren't able to do the same. In fact, when he arrived in New York after his diagnosis, he explained that it would be an insult to Canada to start wearing a coat. Even when traveling in the cold winter weather to cancer treatments, he refused to wear a coat. Some of his fellow Canadians coined this "Doing the Bulka," and a few have shared with our family that they have continued this tradition.

The second identifying aspect of Rabbi Bulka's speeches is that he did not use notes. Rabbi Bulka's father had not used notes either when he delivered sermons; and Rabbi Bulka always felt it was more important to maintain eye contact with the crowd.

The Remembrance Day speech of 1991 was probably one of the first times Rabbi Bulka wrote out his benediction, as he only had 90 seconds to deliver it. Rabbi Bulka used to quote his father, saying, "For speeches of two hours, I need 5 minutes of preparation. For speeches of five minutes, I need two hours of preparation." In fact, many great orators, such as the likes of Mark Twain, have reported similar habits. As a teacher myself, I can attest to this. One hardly needs preparation when there is an unlimited time to speak. However, when one is tasked to convey a meaningful point in a short period of time, preparation is key.

The first speech garnered much positivity from the synagogue's congregants and from Canadians at large. The highest government officials, including the Governor General, Prime Minister, and Minister of Defence, were present at the National War Memorial in 1991, along with thousands of other people at the site and watching at home from their televisions.

From that year forward, Rabbi Bulka delivered the benediction at the National War Memorial on Remembrance Day in Canada as the honorary chaplain of Dominion Command of the Royal Canadian Legion.

Over the years, there were many notable benedictions. In 2007, when many Canadians were deployed in Afghanistan, Rabbi Bulka felt the need to "step up" his address. He was used to leading his congregation back in Alta Vista, and had the entire congregation exclaim "Mazal Tov" (best wishes…) on his count (See Chapter 8). This time, on a much larger scale, Rabbi Bulka instructed the crowd to exclaim: "We love our troops!" They were enthusiastic as they said it, and Remembrance Day of that year was marked by Rabbi Bulka's poignant line and the way he energized the crowd.

Rabbi Bulka felt that there was "an emotional connection" building up. When writing about the event, he said:

> "It struck me that indeed what was evolving was a love for the troops. It was a love that had not yet come to the surface but needed to. So, I asked the 30,000 in attendance to join me in saying: We love our troops. Saying the words brings the feeling forth from the unconscious to the conscious. I then proceeded to say why we love our troops." These were the words:
>
> *We love our troops because of their selflessness.*
>
> *We love our troops because of their unswerving love of Canada.*
>
> *We love our troops because of their bravery and dignity in combat and*
>
> *We love our troops because through them, we gain a more vivid, vital appreciation of all the veterans who fought, on behalf of Canada, for global freedom.*[1]

Through Rabbi Bulka's heartfelt benedictions over thirty years, he personally strengthened the love and appreciation that ordinary Canadians have for our military.

Here is the citation that accompanied Rabbi Bulka's award:

> Canadian Forces Medallion for Distinguished Service is hereby awarded to Rabbi Reuven Bulka, C.M. For many years, Rabbi Bulka has spoken to Canadians from the steps of the National War Memorial in Ottawa, Ontario during the National Remembrance Day ceremonies. His inspiring sermons often underscore the nobility of military service and the sacrifices, both past and present, of Canadian Armed Forces members and their families for our country. Over the years, Rabbi Bulka's venerable presence and

---

1. Bulka, Reuven P., *Old Ideas for New Times*, (Ottawa, Canada, J. Bulka Verlag Publishing House: 2013), 154.

meaningful messages have given comfort to those afflicted by war and conflict and imparted wisdom for understanding and healing. Presented on the 8th of January, 2021, General Jonathan Vance, Chief of Defence staff.

Brigadier General Keith Osmond, speaking directly to Rabbi Bulka in front of his family, explained:

> "This is more than just words given at a Remembrance Day ceremony, sir. Your words came from a place that resonated well with all of the soldiers and their families. They weren't just words, they were meanings that were passed on to us and that we absorbed and we really appreciate it. General Vance personally felt that what you had to say in each of the times that you were asked to speak and you spoke at our memorial was incredible, moving, and he never forgot it and never will."

* * *

On the first Remembrance Day following Rabbi Bulka's passing, Rabbi Bulka posthumously received the Minister of Veterans Affairs Commendation, the highest civilian honor given by the Minister of Veteran Affairs. In fact, there was a public memorial held for Rabbi Bulka before the Remembrance Day ceremony, and even a moment of remembrance at an Ottawa Senators hockey game on the night of November 11.

Why did my grandfather spend so much of his time involved in the military? As a Rabbi, it hardly seems like the first Jewish cause for which one would think to advocate.

Perhaps this excerpt from Frankl can shed light unto his actions:

> "The more one forgets himself – by giving himself to a cause to serve or another person to love – the more human he is and the more he actualizes himself. What is called self-actualization is not an attainable aim at all, for the simple reason that the more one would strive for it, the more he would miss it. In other words, self-actualization is possible only as a side-effect of self-transcendence.[2]

2. Frankl, *Man's Search for Meaning*, 95.

*Pirkay Avot,* too, could shed light onto his involvement in the military. In the very outset of *Pirkay Avot,* it explains that the world stands on three things, one of which is known as "sacred service".[3] In order to become his greatest self, my grandfather understood that it was important to "give himself to a cause to serve." In that way, he would transcend himself, and according to Frankl, would be able to then, as a side effect, be able to achieve self-actualization.

## Chapter 5 – Excerpts and Letters

Remembrance Day 2009:

In the presence of His Royal Highness Prince Charles, whose grandfather, His Majesty King George the Sixth, unveiled this very cenotaph about seventy years ago, we remember the supreme sacrifice that so many beloved Canadians made and were ready to make on land, in the air, at sea: the dead, the wounded, the survivors, the war bereaved men and women, anglophones, francophones, natives, members of a wide range of ethnic and religious communities – we laud and remain in awe of these heroic Canadians.

Heroic Canadians. What does this mean? It means those who went to war on our behalf, putting their lives on hold and at risk in order to eliminate tyranny, defend liberty, and promote freedom, they are world class heroes. As we follow the challenges, the bravery, and the travail of Canadian soldiers presently engaged in ridding the world of the scourge of terrorism at such enormous personal risk, we gain a more complete appreciation of the great heroism of all of our veterans. When we look at our veterans, we are looking at the very best of Canada. Today, indeed every day, our veterans, our heroes deserve to be celebrated, extolled, embraced, thanked, venerated, and applauded. May those who die be remembered lovingly; may those who were injured be healed in body and spirit; may those who served and continue to serve be able to live out their lives in a world free of terror and suffused with tranquility.

We who ride on the coattails of our heroes can best show our gratitude

3. Pirkay Avot 1:2, (Bulka, Ktav Publishing).

by standing up for the values they continue to defend. By nurturing in Canada and enveloping a culture of respect, of harmony, and of conclusion. A great country worthy of their great sacrifice. This is our sacred trust, our unbeatable, unshakeable perpetual obligation. Our way to actively remember. May our embrace of remembrance be a crowning glory for our veterans and our country. Amen.

## LETTER #1

I wish to share with you how meaningful your Remembrance Day services were to my father. My father wasn't particularly religious; however, honouring veterans and acknowledging Remembrance Day were his form of religion (as he grew up on military bases in Canada and overseas). Over the years, he developed a deep respect and admiration for your speeches. You came to be the person he most looked forward to hearing from and he would intently listen to every word you had to say. Your words and message would resonate with my father and he would discuss your speeches after. To be the person my father most respected and wanted to hear from during a military service is the highest compliment my father could give. Thank you for your meaningful services at Remembrance Day. May your days be filled with strength, happiness and peace.

## LETTER #2

Your impact on this world is and will continue to be powerful.

Your spoken and written words have had a healing and powerful effect on me and millions of others world-wide. On Remembrance Day, November 11, 2020, I listened as you spoke to Canada. Part of what you said was that people must be aware of what is happening around them. And should what is being said and done raise troubling feelings, those feelings were not to be merely dismissed.

I am profoundly worried about our beloved Canada. It is being changed drastically and negatively before our very eyes by the 'powers' that be. Yet so many Canadians and others seem to be unaware of what is happening. I firmly believe that you are not one of these individuals.

# *Chapter 6*
# Machzikei Hadas

> "It is a tree of life for those who hold fast to it, and those who uphold it are happy. Its ways are pleasant, and all of its paths peaceful."
>
> – *Genesis 2:9*

Few synagogues around the world have an identifiable coat of arms, and even fewer are recognized by their respective local governments. But Machzikei Hadas is unique in that it is both. It was the first synagogue in the history of the Commonwealth to be granted a coat of arms. As stated on the Machzikei Hadas website:

> The story starts at a dinner party hosted by members of our shul, Linda and Arthur Cogan. In attendance was the Chief Herald of Canada, Robert Watt. When the Cogans found out what Mr. Watt did for a living, they were intrigued. They asked innocently if synagogues could be granted a coat of arms. Mr. Watt replied that there were no rules against doing so. The next day, the Cogans approached Rabbi Bulka and asked for his help in getting an application going. Mr. Watt met with Rabbi Bulka in October of 1992 and the project began.
>
> Before deciding on a design, Mr. Watt wanted to be familiar with Jewish practices and traditions and so attended services and met numerous times with Rabbi Bulka.
>
> The final product combined symbols of Judaism with symbols

> of our synagogue. In the words of Rabbi Bulka, "Machzikei Hadas" literally means "Upholders of the faith." The Torah scroll contains the laws of the faith, and the Ten Commandments represent the foundation of those laws. These symbols are in the crest of the coat of arms. And there are five scrolls to symbolize the Five Books of Moses. In the shul's sanctuary, the Ark containing these scrolls is fronted by beautiful bronze doors designed with a Tree of Life motif by Ottawa sculptor Bruce Garner. Proverbs 3:18 refers to the Torah as a 'tree of life to those who uphold it.' This passage from the Torah is bronzed on the Ark doors. Since it is also reminiscent of the name of the Congregation, "Upholders of the Faith," it is fitting that this verse be the foundation of the coat of arms. Additionally, the tree forms the top of the coat of arms, and on it are attached intermingled maple leaves and Stars of David-Canadian and Jewish symbols. This artistic integration projects the beautiful fusion between Canada and its Jewish community. It expresses the commitment of our synagogue to Canada, and our gratitude to Canada for all it has done for the Jewish community. The Coat of Arms was officially granted in a wonderful ceremony at our shul on November 8, 1994.[4]

* * *

One of the highlights of the Machzikei Hadas experience was the yearly wintertime visits from the eighth graders of Salanter Akiba Riverdale (SAR) Academy in Riverdale, NY. Each year, beginning in 2002, Rabbi Drelich, the principal, would lead the large group of students, which ranged from around 60–100 depending on the year, on a weekend trip to Ottawa.

They would start the trip in the province of Quebec on Thursday morning after having driven up from New York through Wednesday night. They would then arrive in Ottawa, where they would first visit Rabbi Bulka's shul, eat dinner, and meet the Rabbi. Gracious community members invited the students to sleep in their homes

---

4. Congregation Machzikei Hadas, accessed July 10, 2023, https://www.cmhottawa.com/.

for the weekend; and after dinner, they went to their hosts' homes to settle in.

Friday was also jam-packed with activities, including skating and touring Parliament. The students were exhausted by the time the Sabbath arrived at sundown on Friday.

Rabbi Bulka and his congregants were extremely involved in the activities over Shabbos. As Rabbi Drelich put it, "Rabbi Bulka allowed the shul to be the students' classroom." He made sure to speak personally with each student, taught them, joked with them, and made them feel comfortable and at home.

On one occasion, one of the buses that was supposed to leave on Saturday night broke down in the parking lot; and it would be another six hours until a replacement could arrive.

The students had already packed up and moved out of their hosts' homes, so the shul graciously invited the boys to sleep in the building. The next morning, they were given a beautiful breakfast replete with coffee, cereal, and eggs, and Rabbi Bulka himself started scooping eggs onto the students' plates.

The names Rabbi Bulka and Machzikei Hadas go hand in hand. The congregation was like family to him, and in turn, he was family to the congregation. The word "*Machzikei*" in Hebrew means to "take hold of". The Hebrew verse on the shul's coat of arms reads: "*Eitz Chaim Hi Lamachzikim Bah*" – A living tree of Torah, grab hold onto it.

Rabbi Drelich shared a beautiful idea with me that encapsulated my grandfather.

We often read stories about *gedolim* (great people). While they are meant to inspire us, their stories can often leave us feeling inadequate about our own potential. Rabbi Drelich, a friend of my grandfather for decades, pointed out to me that what was so unique about Rabbi Bulka is how human he was.

Rabbi Bulka was relatable. He didn't speak down to people, but instead spoke up. He injected humor into everything he did and made his achievements and greatness look so simple, so attainable. In Rabbi Drelich's words, Rabbi Bulka is someone who was a living example of the *Torah*, but also someone that you can take hold of (*Machzikim bah*), someone that you could look at and say: "Wow, I can become a better person, too."

In fact, at the start of this writing endeavor, this book was just a dream. I've had many dreams prior to this one, and I can't say they've all come to fruition. Once I told my grandfather that I planned to write this book, I realized it was something I had to do. Not because he was adamant about it (he wasn't, he was far too humble to even want a book about his life), but because after interviewing so many people about his life, I started to realize how much he had accomplished and how "within reach" he made it seem. His life is not only what inspired me to write this book, but it's what invigorated me to live out my dream to make it happen.

* * *

So how did Rabbi Bulka become the Rabbi of Congregation Machzikei Hadas?

In 1967, Rabbi Bulka met his beloved late wife, my grandmother, Naomi (of blessed memory). Naomi Jacobovits was from Montreal, but the two of them went out in New York. After just three dates, my grandfather knew that she was "the one," and they became engaged to get married.

At that time, Rabbi Bulka was teaching a seventh grade Talmud class in an elementary school in New York, but he knew that he eventually wanted to go into the rabbinate.

One of the first interviews Rabbi Bulka had was in Rhode Island, in a town a small distance outside of Providence. Rabbi Bulka noticed some flowers sitting atop one of the benches and asked what they were for. He was told it was "the *mechitza*" (partition necessary in Jewish law between men and women in synagogue). It didn't take long for Rabbi Bulka to discover that there was much controversy among the members of the shul regarding the *mechitza*. Rabbi Bulka, astute at the young age of 23, recalled that his instincts told him it was never a good idea to enter a new job on the back of controversy. He respectfully declined the opportunity.

Eventually, something came up in Ottawa, Canada. Rabbi Bulka applied for the job through a placement agency in *Yeshiva Torah V'Daas* and arranged an interview for the position.

It was shortly after the "Three Weeks," a period of mourning during the summer when Jews are not allowed to shave or take a haircut. Ordinarily, Rabbi Bulka would have shaved his beard off completely, but he worried that he'd appear quite young to the interviewer as he was only twenty-three at the time.

It was at that point when Rabbi Bulka's signature goatee was born. In fact, Rabbi Bulka was later told that if not for the goatee, he probably wouldn't have gotten the job.

In true Rabbi Bulka fashion, when his age was brought up at the interview as a possible hindrance to the pulpit position, Rabbi Bulka responded, "I'm going to get older every day, so if you think being older is better, I can promise you I will improve every day."

Rabbi Bulka's job offer coincided with the week after he got married. The day following the last day of *Sheva Brachos* (seven days of celebration following a Jewish wedding), Rabbi Bulka and his wife drove down to Ottawa to start their life together.

They arrived in Ottawa at 3 AM and realized they had no keys. They checked for open doors and ended up climbing in through a side entrance that happened to be opened. Though it wasn't literally a smooth beginning, many good things followed. Little could Rabbi Bulka have known that he would call Ottawa home for over fifty years.

Rabbi Bulka signed a two-year contract for $7,000 per year and a home. The first few years were an adjustment. Given the aging population of the shul, something had to change.

Eventually, one of two choices became inevitable: close the doors of the shul or try to perpetuate the shul in a new neighborhood with more opportunity for membership growth.

This was eerily like the situation that Rabbi Bulka's own father, Rabbi Yaakov Bulka, had dealt with in the Bronx.

Unlike in his father's situation, there was a group of people dedicated to saving the shul from becoming a relic of the past. Rabbi Bulka was invested in the cause and promised the congregants that if there were a viable path to rebuilding the shul in a good neighborhood, he would stick with them. Clearly, he had learned from his own father the importance of the relationship between the Rabbi and congregation.

Just in case this didn't work out, he applied for a few other jobs. Rabbi Bulka found himself interviewing on the West Coast in Seattle at a beautiful shul. He stayed for Shabbos and was promptly offered the position. Rabbi Bulka said he'd have to wait until Monday to accept, as Monday was the day they'd be getting a note from the city of Ottawa to see if the city would buy out the old property so that they'd have a decent down payment for the new property.

After arriving back in Ottawa on Monday, Rabbi Bulka was greeted with the news that the city had agreed to buy the property. Rabbi Bulka called the shul in Seattle and thanked them for the wonderful weekend. He explained, "I made a promise to the people in Ottawa that if it came through, I'd stick with them." Upon recalling this event, Rabbi Bulka explained that the few times he almost left Ottawa were never because he wasn't happy there. In fact, Rabbi Bulka describes his position at Machzikei Hadas as the paradise of Rabbinical positions.

Label Silver *a"h*, a long-time member of Machzikei Hadas, who had been residing in Ottawa even before Rabbi Bulka's arrival and was part of the committee that hired Rabbi Bulka, vividly recalled the initial stages of the synagogue's development:

> During the first Rosh Hashana celebration, the walls of the shul had not yet been constructed. However, the following year marked a significant milestone as the shul opened its doors for Rosh Hashana and Kol Nidrei night, the first evening of Yom Kippur. The turnout was astonishing, with 1100 people filling the space, leaving standing room only. This momentous occasion signifies the beginning of Rabbi Bulka's transformative impact on Ottawa. Through his dedicated efforts, he established a strong foundation for the Jewish community in the city and played a crucial role in preserving Orthodox Judaism in the eastern part of Ottawa.

Rabbi Bulka's true leadership experience began and extended from his Rabbinic position at Machzikei Hadas. Rabbi Bulka's style of leadership was to provide for and be of service for others. Whenever a need arose within the community, Rabbi Bulka promptly took action to address it. Whether it entailed expanding access to kosher food, including setting up a Kosher butcher, or establishing separate girls' and boys' high schools (in addition to serving on the board of a co-ed school), he wholeheartedly embodied the mantra, "In a place where there are no people, strive to be a person".[1] Despite the relatively small Jewish population of around 12,000 in Ottawa when he arrived, Rabbi Bulka succeeded in revitalizing Ottawa's significance within the global Jewry. As Laibel Silver so poignantly remembered: "He laid the foundation for Orthodoxy in Ottawa. He was enjoyable, people flocked to him. You can't find one person in Ottawa who didn't like Rabbi Bulka."

This aligns seamlessly with Frankl's concept of leadership. According to Frankl, "Everyone has his own specific vocation or mission in life; everyone must carry out a concrete assignment that demands fulfillment. Therein he cannot be replaced, nor can his life be repeated. Thus, everyone's task is unique as is his specific opportunity to implement it".[2] Through Rabbi Bulka's vocation as a Rabbi, one can say with certainty that Rabbi Bulka carried out a concrete assignment, one that cannot be replaced. His unwavering dedication and leadership left an indelible mark on the lives of those he served.

## Chapter 6 – Letters

### LETTER #1

I first met Rabbi Bulka after a baseball game in the JMSL (Jewish Men's Softball League). I congratulated him on his new appointment. We chatted and he told me was nervous because he was following Rabbi

---

1. Pirkay Avot 2:5, (Bulka, Ktav Publishing).
2. Frankl, *Man's Search for Meaning*, 93.

Eckstein, who had served the community for so long, and now he was the new rookie in town. I can say with conviction that the rookie turned out to be a "legend in the community."

## LETTER #2

A Miracle Hidden in Plain Sight?

A year or two ago, I was chatting with Rabbi Bulka and told him that our family had benefited enormously from the shul. Our children saw how much shul members valued family and community. When our children established their own families and joined new communities, those values stuck.

Rabbi Bulka's achievement is more than it seems. We all know families that squabble and shul communities that split into bickering factions. For Rabbi Bulka to have sustained a harmonious community for fifty years is an extraordinary achievement. It is arguably a miracle hidden in plain sight that benefitted literally thousands of people. He achieves this feat by adhering to the commandment "Love your neighbor as yourself" – the pinnacle of kindness.

Rabbi Sacks collected data explaining the importance of community. He showed that people who regularly attend a house of worship commit to "collective responsibility for the common good" and have birth rates capable of sustaining populations. Sadly, he noted that much of the Western world has steadily abandoned religious observance and now confronts faltering demographics and bizarre morals defined without reference to community.

Of course, Rabbi Bulka's approach to community has always been intensely practical. It covers, for example, shul, acts of kindness, interfaith initiatives, blood donation, cancer treatment and organ transplant. However, I'd venture to suggest that building a harmonious and sustained community – the possible miracle hidden in plain sight-ranks high in comparison with these other great achievements.

## LETTER #3

Although we belong to another Synagogue, Rabbi Bulka treats us as his congregants. He has reached out to us in our times of need and compassion and rejoices with us in our simchas. His selflessness and dedication to tikkun olam is widely known. When we travel abroad and touch base with Jewish communities, we are amazed by how many people ask about Rabbi Bulka when we mention our Ottawa Connection.

## LETTER #4

I first met Rabbi Bulka in 1972 in his study at the Murray Street Shul. I was looking for some direction at that point in my life. We weren't members of Machzikei Hadas, but my mother thought I would relate better to a young, more approachable Rabbi. She was right, and our discussion led me to making important decisions. Through the years, I enjoyed my conversations with Rabbi Bulka. He was always approachable, and I enjoyed his sense of humour.

## LETTER #5

My family's memories of Rabbi Bulka are meaningful ones that provide us with positive thoughts always. My first introduction to Rabbi Bulka was through my late husband. He considered Rabbi Bulka one of his dearest friends and he had so much admiration and respect for him. They worked on many projects together both in the Ottawa Jewish Community and at Carleton University. Having met the Rabbi, I knew he was the one to Bar Mitzvah my son. In order to get to know him better, the Rabbi found out about his love for sports; so, he made a point of getting to know him on the baseball field. The two of them played catch for quite a while while chatting and the Rabbi was able to get a good sense of who my son was.

Rabbi Bulka also got to know my daughter in an academic sense. At University she was writing a paper on Ottawa Jewish Cemeteries and the two of them traipsed through the snow to visit these historical sites. It was the Rabbi who educated her on the importance of these sites. When my beloved husband passed away and I chose to bury him in Toronto, it was Rabbi Bulka who flew to Toronto to conduct the funeral and later, his unveiling.

Over the years, Rabbi Bulka has kept in touch with me to see how I was doing.

Rabbi Bulka is and continues to be one of the finest, kindest, knowledgeable people my family has ever known. He is "the" example of what a Rabbi should be to his community, his worshippers and to all individuals he serves. We send him our prayers for comfort, strength and gratitude for his friendship and guidance.

### LETTER #7

About a year after Rabbi Bulka arrived in Ottawa in the late 1960s, he invited my parents and us four children to a seder at his home. We lived a block away from each other in Sandy Hill. I was 16 years old, and I had never been to a seder like that before and have never been to one like that since. I remember that almost every page of the Haggadah led to some lengthy and animated discussion about Biblical passages, Rabbinic interpretations, talmudic tracts, ethics, Jewish history, Kabalistic decoding, modern-day Haggadah variations and the differences between the Sephardic and Ashkenazi Passover traditions. Somewhere in-between we managed to read the Haggadah, sing, eat, bench, laugh and bless our good fortune. I recall we left after two in the morning. As we walked home, I remember my head, heart, stomach, and spirit were very full. Thank you to Rabbi Bulka and your family!

*Chapter 7*

# Softballs and Hospitals

> "In everyone's life, at some time, our inner fire goes out. It is then burst into flame by an encounter with another human being. We should all be thankful for those people who rekindle the inner spirit."
>
> – *Albert Schweitzer*

Rabbi Bulka was visiting a congregant's mother in the hospital, as was his general practice when a congregant's family member was sick. The woman did not have her own room and was sharing the hospital space with another woman, someone who was a stranger to Rabbi Bulka.

Being who he was, Rabbi Bulka intuited that this woman was lonely as she did not have any visitors. After that, each time Rabbi Bulka visited his congregant's mother, he also made it his business to spend some time with her roommate.

Soon, the congregant's mother was released from the hospital, but her roommate was not. In typical Rabbi Bulka fashion, my grandfather continued to visit this woman in the hospital until she was eventually released.

One might think there could be ulterior motives behind a shul Rabbi visiting the sick in the hospital, but as this woman was not even Jewish and therefore had no chance of joining Rabbi Bulka's congregation, this would be far from the truth. Rabbi Bulka never took advantage of the vulnerable. He did not want to build on the backs of anyone else.

If a current member ever contemplated leaving the shul for personal reasons, Rabbi Bulka counseled him or her with no ulterior motive. A former shul member confided that following a difficult divorce, he was considering moving to Toronto and wanted the Rabbi's input. After listening and understanding the member's circumstances, Rabbi Bulka told him it was absolutely in his best interest to move to Toronto, even if it would leave the shul with one less member.

My grandfather recalled that he visited with people in the hospital regularly, and that it didn't matter who it was. It was rewarding to visit people, and it's where Rabbi Bulka forged so many important relationships. Even after they returned home, Rabbi Bulka called them daily until they recovered. One person joked that after her surgery, Rabbi Bulka sent sweets to her house and called every day for two weeks. At a certain point, she said, "Rabbi, even my mother stopped calling me at this point," but Rabbi Bulka was not deterred.

Rabbi Bulka recalled joking with his father that in terms of visiting congregants in the hospital, living in Ottawa was a blessing. My grandfather's father, Rabbi Yaakov Bulka, was a Rabbi in the Bronx. Visiting the sick was harrowing for him because his congregants were scattered in all different hospitals around the New York Metropolitan area. Anyone who has ever driven in New York City can also appreciate the difficulties of parking. It could take my great-grandfather so long just to find a parking spot that he'd be fortunate to have visited one hospital in a three-hour time span.

Rabbi Bulka dubbed it a blessing to live in Ottawa because in three hours, he could visit every person in every hospital in Ottawa. In fact, the hospital staff in Ottawa liked the idea of clergy visits so much that they gave Rabbi Bulka complimentary parking, which made things much smoother.

My grandfather looked back at those visits and recalled that they were some of the most meaningful connections he made with people.

> "They weren't all so pleasant, though," he explained. "I once knocked on a door and a woman said, 'I didn't ask for a Rabbi, I don't want to see you. Get out of here.' It was a good wake up

call for me, not to take for granted that just because you want to see them, it doesn't mean they would like to see you. After this, I made sure to tell the patients I visited, 'Please let me know when you want me to leave, and I'm gone.'"

In other words, Rabbi Bulka understood the true purpose of visiting others. While it might seem obvious, the goal of visiting the sick is to lift their spirits, to encourage them, to make them feel energized. As Rabbi Bulka put it, "The visit is about them. If you lose sight of that, you may as well stay home."

Upon reflecting on his hospital visits, Rabbi Bulka exclaimed, "There were some meaningful, sobering experiences. You'd have to be stupid not to gain lessons from it."

Together with hospital visits, softball games were up there with the most important way of forging connections with community members and congregants. Rabbi Bulka crushed the stereotypes of a shul Rabbi. He recalled winning a few championships over the years and having wonderful experiences with different teams over the course of time.

> "One year, I had a particularly good year. I remember we were playing a game and we were getting crushed. So the pitcher gave up and asked, 'Does anyone want to pitch?' So I said, 'What's the difference, I'll try it.' So I did it for the first time. I threw it over the plate, and pitched a no-hitter that day. I could not have predicted that this was something I could do. But I guess I did well enough that I got the job as the team's pitcher. In fact, one year, I did so well that I was named the MVP of the entire league.
>
> I really enjoyed it, but most importantly, I met so many people. It was interesting, because some of the people I met may never have ended up going to Shul or meeting a Rabbi. I ended up marrying off many of them."

Softball games and hospital visits were two of the most effective ways that Rabbi Bulka said helped his shul grow, albeit unintentionally. Rabbi Bulka was clear that he would not use either of these as an opportunist, but simply as a means of forming and maintaining connections with people throughout the greater Ottawa community. In embodying the essence of *Pirkay Avot*'s imperative, "Let all who occupy themselves with the community do so for the sake of Heaven,"[1] Rabbi Bulka exemplified a profound devotion to a higher purpose, acting with a sense of divine calling and dedication to God in all of his endeavors.

> "In many shuls, there are big events created with the hopes of bringing in new members, and any of those initiatives are of course worthwhile and worth pursuing. But the most important thing is that if something is done naturally without pressure and without a hidden agenda, that's probably the best way to establish relationships.
>
> I played baseball because I enjoyed it, and I visited hospitals because I grew up with the idea that this is one of the *mitzvot* (commandments) that are of utmost importance. I would never have imagined that these would be two things that made such an enormous impact."

In setting up the shul in Ottawa and engaging with the congregation in softball, and through visiting congregants in the hospital, Rabbi Bulka exemplified logotherapy in action.

As Frankl wrote:

> Don't aim at success. The more you aim at it and make it a target, the more you are going to miss it. For success, like happiness, cannot be pursued; it must ensue, and it only does so as the unintended side effect of one's personal dedication to a cause greater than oneself or as the by-product of one's surrender to a person other than oneself. Happiness must happen, and the same holds for success: you have to let it happen by not caring about it. I want you to listen to what your conscience commands you to do and go on to carry it out to the best of your knowledge. Then you will live to see that in the long-run – in the long-run, I

1. Pirkay Avot 2:2, (Bulka, Ktav Publishing).

say! – success will follow you precisely because you had forgotten to think about it.[2]

The growth of his shul in Ottawa, perhaps, was my grandfather's largest accomplishment in his lifetime. Rabbi Bulka's relationship and connection to his congregants knew no bounds. The way in which he would drop anything to attend a funeral of a congregant truly showed his dedication to his shul. But to grow it, he did not poach people, and he did not pressure anyone. He simply let it happen "by not caring about it," and instead listened to what his conscience demanded of him (Frankl). He enjoyed playing softball with fellow shul members, and so that is what he did. He felt a calling to visit congregants in the hospital, and so he made those visits a priority. Success followed him, as Frankl would say, precisely because he "had forgotten to think about it."

If you look at the letters that follow, you will see just how great an impact Rabbi Bulka's hospital visits and softball games had.

## Chapter 7 – Letters

### LETTER #1

My late parents were very sick for 5 years before they died. They were in and out of hospitals frequently. When in hospital, a member of our immediate family would stay with the sick parent on a 24/7 basis. Rabbi Bulka was always around at the hospitals. I never understood how he could just show up and how he could do this for all of us. He was always there. Eighteen months after my late Father passed, my late Mother died at home one day in the early afternoon. Rabbi Bulka's comforting words to our immediate family were 'You guys wrote the book on Honour thy Mother and thy Father.' That was 15 years ago and the memory of those well-picked words will stay with me forever.

### LETTER #2

Every year a group of Ottawa men and women would get together on the weekend in the early 1990s to raise money for the Children's Hospital

2. Frankl, *Man's Search for Meaning*, 9.

of Eastern Ontario (CHEO) by playing 12 consecutive two-hour softball games against other teams (firefighters, students, local companies, even CHEO staff). The event was called CHARITHON and it raised close to a million dollars for the hospital.

At daybreak on Sunday, Rabbi Bulka, who was a pitcher of some renown, would gather together at least 10 of the Jewish male players and have a morning service (Shacharit) right beside the first base line.

For many of us, it was a chance to pause from one worthy endeavour to perform another mitzvah (good deed). There was something very special about praying early morning out in the open, and Rabbi Bulka ensured that we concentrated on our davening (praying).

We must have looked quite strange to the others dressed in our baseball uniforms, but with tallit (prayer shawl) and tephillin (phylacteries) as well.

Truly a highlight for all of us thanks to our wonderful Rabbi.

### LETTER #3

During my grandmother's shiva, my father and his brothers decided to get Rabbi Bulka a new softball glove. It was presented to him with thanks and the hope that the glove would be part of the winning team for the upcoming softball season.

Graciously thanking them, Rabbi Bulka asked if they knew how to properly break in a new glove. With a twinkle in his eye, he threw the glove on the floor and began jumping up and down on it, saying, "This is how I break in a new glove!"

My young daughter had been watching, and when retelling the day's events later that night, said "'Manjump' had come to her Bubby and Zaideh's house. No amount of persuasion could change this for her. Rabbi Bulka was now Manjump in her world.

We all, Rabbi included, had a good laugh about the name and its origins, and he bore the name with good humour.

Manjump was a brief interval, and I was a little sad when the inevitable evolution came and Manjump became Rabbi Bulka once again.

As our Rabbi, he traveled with us through life's cycles. He guided and supported us through births/deaths, weddings/funerals and all the other celebrations/challenges presented to us. An email from him saying, "Haven't heard from you in a while. Checking in to see how you are," was a steadying comfort. His presence throughout my life has been a cherished and invaluable one.

And what was our role to play in all this? What were our obligations to continue successfully? Rabbi Bulka's instructions are succinct and direct – be kind and do good.

I once took pause that the direction from an Orthodox Rabbi was not "Be a good Jew" but "Be a good person," but it should never have surprised me. His flock does not just involve his congregants, or members of his faith. We are all charged with the same simple directives to make our own individual and global worlds a better place.

## LETTER #4

As a newlywed couple moving to Ottawa on our own without any family, we found a wonderful extended family at Machzikei Hadas Congregation. Rabbi Bulka personally greeted us at every service or class we attended. Rabbi Bulka was the first person to see our newborn daughter in the hospital. This was not a unique or unusual occurrence for Rabbi Bulka because Rabbi Bulka made it his trademark to visit people in hospital on a daily basis. We certainly felt very special and Rabbi Bulka made it very special by constantly reminding us how he was the first visitor.

Rabbi Bulka's relationship with our daughter continued. When I couldn't find a babysitter so that I could attend Rabbi Bulka's Tuesday morning women's class, Rabbi Bulka encouraged me to bring our baby daughter to class. Not only was she a welcome participant, but by the end of class she typically found herself sitting on Rabbi Bulka's lap as he wrapped up the class. Our relationship with Rabbi Bulka endured even after our departure from Ottawa. We met each other at conferences and lectures he gave and his thoughtfulness was most welcome when we received a personal email inquiring how we were managing at the height of the Covid pandemic.

## LETTER #5

I was brought up by an atheist mother and a traditionally Jewish father. The only exposure I had to religion growing up in Montreal was my Bar Mitzvah, going to synagogue once a year for the High Holy Days and having Passover Seders with family friends. Rabbis were serious and scary people.

After moving to Ottawa in 1977, I joined the Jewish Men's Softball League and Rabbi Bulka was our team's pitcher. Thanks to him, it did not take long for my image of Rabbis to be shattered and my meaningful Jewish journey to begin in earnest. It was his unique ability to be both a revered Rabbi and "one of the guys" that attracted me and so many others to his flock.

God knows I had and still have a lot to learn about our religion and Rabbi Bulka has always been there to kindly and patiently guide and mentor me. Never any pressure. He "met me at all times where I was" and helped lead me to where I needed to be.

In my late father's twilight years, he used to join me in Ottawa for the High Holy Days. On our way home from synagogue, he would always say "that Rabbi Bulka, he's one in a million!" I am sorry to disagree, Dad, but the denominator is much more than that!

Thank you eternally, dearest Rabbi, for igniting the spark in my Jewish soul that burns ever so brightly!

## LETTER #6

He literally saved my life. I had a major cancer operation and was wheeled down the hall to the operating room in the hospital and I looked behind me and I saw my wife and Rabbi Bulka. For 18 months of chemo, he literally took care of me. He came every day to the hospital at 7 AM in the morning. He would drive my wife to the hospital.

# *Chapter 8*

# 1-2-3 Mazal Tov!

"Life is not a matter of milestones, but moments."

– *Rose Kennedy*

The word "impossible" simply was not in Rabbi Bulka's vocabulary when it came to attending a *simcha* (celebration of a happy milestone). If there were enough physical hours to attend, you could be sure Rabbi Bulka would be there.

*Erev Sukkot,* the Jewish Holiday of Huts, fell out on a Sunday. It was of incredible importance to Rabbi Bulka that he be with his congregants in Ottawa for the holiday.

Meanwhile, Rabbi Bulka needed to be in New York for a family celebration taking place the morning before the beginning of the holiday.

There were no options to fly because flights were not available after the celebration that would return him to Ottawa on time for the holiday. Since flying wasn't an option, Rabbi Bulka decided he would drive to New York from Ottawa overnight, arrive in the morning, attend the celebration, and return to Ottawa by car immediately following the celebration to make it back to Ottawa by sundown that evening.

When the shul president got word of Rabbi Bulka's plan, he said, "No way am I letting you do that. I will hire you a limo driver to take you back so that you will be able to rest." After some back and forth, Rabbi Bulka reluctantly agreed to the president's plan.

As far as everyone knew, Rabbi Bulka arrived in New York, attended the celebration, and returned to Canada via a limo driver, exactly as planned.

It was more than ten years later that the shul president told us the real story.

Rabbi Bulka was driven to the celebration without a problem, and the limo driver took a nap during the festivities. Afterwards, Rabbi Bulka entered the backseat of the limo, resting before the Sukkot holiday. About three hours into the trip, the driver pulled into a rest area to sleep.

"What are you doing?" my grandfather asked.

"I'm tired," the driver responded, "I simply can't drive anymore."

My grandfather explained that he had to be home by sundown. When the limo driver insisted on his inability to drive, Rabbi Bulka said, "No problem, I will drive." The driver explained that he would get into huge trouble with his employer if he allowed someone else to drive his limo. Rabbi Bulka responded by explaining how important it was for him to arrive back in Canada before the holiday. Anyone who knew Rabbi Bulka knew that it was nearly impossible to say no to him. Eventually, the driver relented. Rabbi Bulka made sure to don the full limo gear, equipped with the special driver's hat, when they arrived at the border. Or at least that is the legend. He drove the entire rest of the way home while the limo driver slept in the back.

When Rabbi Bulka arrived in Ottawa, he felt obligated to tell the shul president, David Freeman (a.k.a. Moose), about the ordeal, considering the limo had been paid for by the shul. My grandfather made the president promise not to tell the story for "a long time" so as not to get the limo driver in trouble. Hence, we only discovered the story so many years later.

This story personifies Rabbi Bulka in so many ways.

Most obviously, it is evident that my grandfather would do whatever it took to be there for his family and their milestones while still being there for his congregation. He was dedicated to his family, and he was dedicated to his second family, Machzikei Hadas.

It also highlights his incredible sense of humor and his ability to influence people.

Most of all, the story illustrates his sensitivity. This would have been a great story to tell, but most people never heard it because he refused to tell it for fear that it would get the limo driver in trouble.

One might not think that attendance at milestones is of utmost importance. How many of us groan when we are invited to an event because of the hassle of travel it will inevitably entail? Rabbi Bulka was dedicated to being there for people at all of their milestones and celebrating them with the congregation.

On occasion, when Rabbi Bulka had a wedding in Israel, he would fly into the airport, hop into a cab, attend the wedding, and head straight back to the airport. He was determined to be there for the important milestones in people's lives, and he was equally determined to be back in Ottawa for his congregation. He lived the mantra "Do not consider anything impossible, for there is no person who does not have an hour and no thing that does not have its place".[3]

In fact, there likely isn't a grandchild of Rabbi Bulka's, pre-Covid, that was not visited in the hospital upon their birth. Even if it meant driving eight hours through the night, he was determined to be there. Even for more distant family members, Rabbi Bulka was known to call without an introduction. He would launch straight into an exuberant "Mazal Tov!" and family members would quickly understand who was on the other end of the phone line.

I personally recall my grandfather's hospital visit when I gave birth to my first child. He drove in to be there following the birth. I recall being in a lot of pain when my grandfather came to visit, as I had given birth via cesarean. Even though Rabbi Bulka had traveled far to be there for this occasion, he was equally content when I told him it was hard for me to entertain visitors at that time. Once again, Rabbi Bulka didn't do good deeds to check off a box. He did it for the person on the receiving end of his kind act.

Anyone that has traveled to Rabbi Bulka's shul in Ottawa will recall his famous "1-2-3 Mazal Tov" that he said at the end of Shabbos *davening* (prayers) each week. When announcing the happy occasions

3. Pirkay Avot 4:3, (Bulka, Ktav Publishing).

that happened in shul, my grandfather exclaimed: "1-2-3," and the entire congregation responded in a roar of "Mazal Tovs." Not only did Rabbi Bulka try to be in attendance at milestones, but he ensured that everyone celebrated them and gave them the excitement they deserved.

I often listen to a voicemail that I have saved from my grandfather that he left me after I delivered my first baby. The excitement in his voice was palpable. He managed to leave a short voicemail replete with a signature Rabbi Bulka pun, excitement, and good wishes. He usually ended phone calls or voicemails with: "*Zei Gezunt un Shtark*," Yiddish for: "Be healthy and strong."

It wasn't just happy occasions that my grandfather made an effort to attend. Almost every one of Rabbi Bulka's children can recall a moment where they had to turn back from a vacation or trip because their father had gotten a call that there was a *levaya* (funeral) to attend. In fact, funerals were such a normal part of their lives that instead of playing the typical "house" that children play, they played "funeral," beginning with the fancy car that would come to the house and pick them up to attend the service.

In 1983, Rabbi Bulka and his family went to Israel for a year on sabbatical. While everyone else stayed in the county throughout the year, Rabbi Bulka traveled back and forth several times from Israel to Canada, even staying in Canada to be with his congregation for the high holidays.

There were times that Rabbi Bulka's children resented their father's constant attendance at funerals and weddings, sometimes to the detriment of their own time with him. Ironically, Rabbi Bulka himself had the same "complaint" about his own father. In retrospect, though, they understand why it was so important to him.

So many of the emails that came in after Rabbi Bulka's diagnosis was announced revolved around the idea that Rabbi Bulka was always in attendance at the best and worst of times in each of the writers' lives. I have attached a few poignant emails to give another voice attesting to this special attribute of Rabbi Bulka.

When my grandfather recounted his memories with Viktor Frankl, he remembers Frankl telling him that he absolutely hated going to cocktail parties because it was a waste of time and involved too much small talk. I wondered if my grandfather felt similarly to Frankl. While he attended every event, he did not always stay long. It seems to me, in retrospect, that if he had the opportunity to attend two events, each for a shorter time, he would have chosen that option over attending one event for a longer period. Perhaps the reason for this, considering logotherapeutic ideas, was because he attempted to use each moment of his life to find meaning. If he felt like his presence was no longer meaningful, or if he felt that his presence would be more meaningful at a different event, he would sometimes leave early. But he seemed to know which events to stay at for their duration, such as the weddings of his grandchildren, because he knew that at those milestones, his presence alone would be meaningful.

## Chapter 8 – Letters

### LETTER #1

Murray and I were engaged to be married in the summer of 1968. The Rabbi who was to marry us was now going to be out of town. He asked Reverend Schreiber who had been a neighbour and a big part of the Shul I went to growing up. He was hesitant and asked the new Rabbi in Ottawa to officiate.

A month before the date my mother had a coronary. Rabbi Bulka made all the arrangements for us to be married in the First Pavilion South sunroom at the Civic Hospital, arriving with a Chuppah for our brothers to hold. We were married on August 11, 1968 and my mother, still in hospital, was able to be there with us.

It was the beginning of many years of Rabbi Bulka being an important part of many events in our family for which we are very grateful.

### LETTER #2

When my Mother became critically ill and was in the ICU at the General, I called Rabbi Bulka because my sisters and I were not sure what to do. My Mother was hanging on to life and would not let go. My Mother was raised Orthodox but my Father, who already passed, was raised Reform. Out of love and respect for our Mother, we wanted things to be done properly. We always were members of Machzikei Hadas, because my Mother's family were part of the group that started the synagogue on Murray street. We have known Rabbi Bulka since the first day he became our Rabbi.

The day I called, he was driving back from New York after visiting his family. He came directly to the hospital instead of going home first. The young resident in charge was a member of our synagogue. Rabbi Bulka went in to see my Mother with the doctor and we waited in the waiting room. When he came out, he told us to go home and they would call us if anything changed. My Mother died before my sisters and I got home. She always tried to protect us from sadness and suffering throughout our lives and was not about to change on her last day of life.

At the funeral, Rabbi Bulka let my sisters and myself do the prayers at her grave site, even though we were women. He told us people will question this, but he told us to tell them it was the right thing to do.

We will always be grateful for Rabbi Bulka's kindness and compassion towards us during this difficult time. He is a true Humanitarian and mentor for us all.

## LETTER #3

I first met you when I gave birth to Ilana at the Civic campus in 1985. I was so honoured to meet you.

Our paths crossed when I began working at Hillel Lodge down on Wurtemburg St. We were so happy to have you take the time from your busy days and spread a lot of cheer with the residents. When you said you would come, we knew we would see you! You put lots of smiles on faces! Then I started working at Star of David and had the pleasure of your company on a weekly basis. You would visit the classes, give a smile and everyone felt so good. We decorated the Sukkah, planted trees, made matza and graduated, all with your encouragement. Jeremy and Ilana felt very connected to you. After their graduations from Star of David, they did their volunteer hours tutoring in the school.

It continues with Ilana celebrating her Bat Mitzvah at Machzikei Hadas. Ilana and Nate were married by you, once at Hillel Lodge, so that my mom could attend. You were very gracious. You then completed the wedding helping out in the kitchen as we, Eric, Claire-Jehanne and I prepared the food for the wedding in Chelsea, Quebec. You married Ilana and Nate again in Chelsea. It was a beautiful wedding!

I was blown away when you called me in Montreal when my mom passed away. It was so kind and thoughtful. You made us feel so special during such a difficult time.

Most recently you drove from Ottawa to my sister's home in Toronto to be at the bris of Ilana and Nate's son, Moe! And then you drove right back to Ottawa! You are one energetic and thoughtful man! I am so proud to have had the pleasure of your presence in my life!

### LETTER #4

I will never forget the kindness that Rabbi Bulka showed when he took time out of a trip to Vancouver to make a shiva call for my late father. I was nine months pregnant at the time and living in Ottawa and my father had passed away in Vancouver. Fortunately I was able to travel to see my father before his death, and thanks to technology, was able to stay closely connected via video. Nonetheless, not being with my family for shiva was incredibly difficult. Not only did Rabbi Bulka walk me through shiva on my own, he physically went to the shiva house on my behalf. It still brings tears of gratitude to my eyes when I think about it seven years later. One. Two. Three. Todah Rabah!

### LETTER #5

Rabbi Bulka has been part of our lives in so many ways over the years, but there are two particular stories that I would like to share.

Just over 29 years ago we went on a family trip to Israel with Rabbi Bulka, our daughter and both sets of our parents. One morning we had planned to leave on our bus at 8 AM sharp to start our journey. I noticed my then 80-year-old father and mother were nowhere to be found. They finally came downstairs at 8 AM when we were scheduled to leave, and

Rabbi Bulka being the intuitive and caring person he is, sat down at the breakfast table with them, not wanting them to feel badly about holding up the trip. Eight months later my dear father passed away from cancer. After the funeral, I received a call from Rabbi Bulka. What was most touching about this call, was that his dear wife Naomi was dying in the hospital in Baltimore from cancer. She died 1 week later. This truly portrays the caring nature and character of Rabbi Bulka, reaching out to me, all whilst he was dealing with his own personal devastation.

I will never forget his kindness. Thank you for all that you have done for our family. You truly are one of a kind!

## LETTER #6

I have been influenced by many, but none as consistently as Rabbi Bulka. I first got to know him when I was 12 years old, and started attending Machzikei Hadas, which was close to my home in Ottawa, but not my family's synagogue. I was immediately welcomed into the synagogue community. During my high school years, as I was becoming more committed to Orthodoxy, and lacked a peer group of like-minded people, he was there for me. I attended his Monday night Talmud class from 1975–1980 – I was about half the age of the average attendee, but Rabbi Bulka made me feel like one of the gang. During my lengthy search for a spouse, he was there to encourage me. During my two stints in Yeshiva in Israel, he dropped in to visit me. He stood under the chuppah with Tzippy and me as the mesader kiddushin in 1992. During my father's illness, he was there for me. I recall walking over to his home in 1996, about an hour after my father's passing, for advice and comfort. During my battles with cancer, he would check in frequently to see how I was doing. He was there for me and my family during my mother's slow slide into the fog of Alzheimers. Two years ago, when my mother collapsed on the street at my cousin's funeral, he stopped the procession and made sure that everything was under control until the EMS arrived.

*Shmuel's Bar Mitzvah · Bulka Family Photo*

*In Vienna with Viktor Frankl and his wife, Eleonore "Elly" Katharina Schwindt · Frankl Family Photo*

*With late wife, Naomi. December 1990 · Bulka Family Photo*

*Jewish Men's Softball League · Photo by Irving Osterer*

*Jewish Men's Softball League · Photo by Irving Osterer*

*With Israeli Prime Minister Shimon Peres · Bulka Family Photo*

*With Canadian Prime Minister Brian Mulroney · Bulka Family Photo*

*Coat of Arms for Machzikei Hadas · Picture provided by Machzikei Hadas*

*With Ron Prehogan at opening of Irving & Shirley Greenberg Cancer centre at Queensway Carleton Hospital. May 2010 · Photo by Peter Waiser*

*With Dan Greenberg and wife Barbara Crook at Queensway Carleton when they dedicated Irving & Shirley Greenberg Cancer centre at Queensway Carleton Hospital. May 2010 · Photo by Peter Waiser*

*Tribute to Rabbi Bulka at Ottawa Senators game at the Canadian Tire Centre for Remembrance Day (Nov 11, 2021) · Bulka Family Photo*

*Canadian Forces Medallion for Distinguished Service · L-R (Deputy Military Advisor Major Rick Cameron, Canada's Ambassador to the United Nations Ambassador Robert Rae, Rabbi Bulka, Brigadier-General Keith Osmond) · Bulka Family Photo*

*Serving eggs to the* SAR *(Salanter Akiba Riverdale Academy) eighth graders · Photo by Rabbi Moshe Drelich*

CONGREGATION MACHZIKI ADAS
259 Murray Street
Ottawa 2, Ontario

August 22, 1967

Dear Member:

We know that our congregation will appreciate and enjoy meeting

RABBI REUBEN BULKA

who will be officiating in our synagogue this coming weekend, August 25 to 27, as an applicant for the position of spiritual leader.

Rabbi Bulka is a native of New York where he received his religious and secular education, which resulted in his receiving his Bachelor of Arts Degree from the City College of New York, and his rabbinical ordination from Rabbi Jacob Joseph Rabbinical Seminary.

Please do take advantage of exposing yourself to a variety in personalities, which our synagogue has arranged for you, your wife, and youth from twelve years up. Do not miss this wonderful chance of meeting a dynamic, orthodox, young Rabbi.

The Shabbat-and weekend-schedule are as follows:

Friday, August 25 Mincha 7:25 P.M.
Shabbat, August 26 Morning Services 8:45 A.M.
Sermon by Rabbi Bulka 10:30 A.M.
Service conclude 11:30 A.M. followed by Kiddush
Talmud Class by Rabbi Bulka 7:00 P.M. followed by Mincha Services 7:45 P.M. and learning of Pirkeh-Avoth
Maariv 8:45 P.M.
Sunday, August 26 Morning Services 9:00 A.M.
Breakfast and address by Rabbi Bulka 9:45 A.M.
Question and Answer Period

Sincerely yours,

Bert Koenig, Ritual Chairman
R. Appotive, President

*Notice to Machzikei Hadas membership, announcing weekend proba (Rabbinical tryout) of Rabbi Bulka*

*With Label Silver, Harry Prizant, Shmuel Prizant at Shmuel Prizant Bar Mitzvah. April 26, 2010 · Photo by Peter Waiser*

*Receiving the order of Canada with his wife, Leah, his children and Governor General of Canada David Johnston, May 7, 2014 · Bulka Family photo*

*Hockey game: Ottawa Senators vs San Hose Sharks.*
*October 27, 2019 · Photo by Dan Greenberg*

*With all of his children at his grandson's Bar Mitzvah.*
*January 2020 · Bulka Family photo*

*Key to the city of Ottawa Reception. February 18, 2010 · Bulka Family photo*

*With members of Parliament on Parliament Hill.*
*November 27, 2013 · Photo by Peter Waiser*

*With Ottawa Mayor Jim Watson. June 17, 2007 · Photo by Peter Waiser*

*With grandson, Avi Bulka at inauguration of Rabbi Bulka Kindness Park. October 27, 2019 · Bulka Family Photo*

*Start of Kindness week at Accora Village, February 15, 2018 · Photo by Peter Waiser*

*Kindness Week with Mayor Jim Watson and MP Lisa McLeod. February 14, 2019 · Photo by Peter Waiser*

PRIME MINISTER · PREMIER MINISTRE

Ottawa, Ontario
K1A 0A2

June 15, 2021

Dear Rabbi Bulka and Senator Munson:

I would like to congratulate you both on Bill S-223: *An Act respecting Kindness Week* receiving royal assent on June 3, 2021. Your support was instrumental in its passage, and making Canada the first country to put Kindness Week into law.

In times of difficulties, like what we face now in our society, we need the opportunity to reflect on what unites us and not on what divides us. That is why Kindness Week will be such an integral part of our country because of its ability to bring us together to support and cherish each other. Being kind to those around you has the power to reverberate good actions in every school, every workplace, every institution, and in every corner of our country. With every act of kindness, we have the undeniable ability to change a town, a city, a province, a territory, a country, and even the world for the better.

Senator Munson, thank you for supporting this Bill in the Senate and for advocating for this important week. You presented a strong voice in a much-needed moment, and your leadership was profound. I would also like to take the opportunity to wish you all the best in your upcoming retirement from the Senate.

Rabbi Bulka, I know that you continue to face your battle with cancer, but the strength and courage that you have shown, has not only inspired me, but all Canadians who have come to look to you for guidance during challenging periods. Kindness Week would not be possible without you, and on behalf of everyone in Canada, thank you. Words can never fully encapsulate the magnitude and impact that you have had on so many lives.

Please accept my warmest regards.

Sincerely,

Rabbi Reuven Bulka
The Honourable Jim Munson, Senator

*Letter from the Prime Minister, offering congratulations on Kindness Week becoming part of Canadian law · Office of the Prime Minister*

*With Israeli Chief Rabbi David Lau, 2018 · Photo by Alex Sarna*

*Extended family at son Shmuel's Bar Mitzvah · Bulka Family Photo*

*Multi Faith service with US Ambassador Paul Celucci, Israeli Ambassador Haim Divon, Gerry Levitz, Honourable Herb Gray. February 4, 2003 · Photo by Peter Waiser*

*With former Ottawa Mayor Larry O'Brien. Key to city ceremony. February 18, 2010 · Bulka Family Photo*

*With Daniel Alfredsson, former captain of the Ottawa Senators. December 2014 · Photo by Dan Greenberg*

*Holocaust remembrance service at Canadian War Museum. April 12, 2010 · Photo by Peter Waiser*

*Bulka family with Canadian Prime Minister Stephen Harper.*
*October 2, 2009 · Office of the Prime Minister · Photo by Deb Ransom*

*With shul Cantors, Chazzanim Weissbord and Levinson · Bulka Family Photo*

*Presentation to his son Eliezer at his Bar Mitzvah (December 1990) · Bulka Family Photo*

*With his father, Rabbi Yaakov Bulka, at the bris of his son Shmuel · Bulka Family Photo*

*With Israeli Prime Minister Yitzchak Shamir · Bulka Family Photo*

*Protesting on behalf of Russian Jewry · Bulka Family Photo*

*With Rabbi Scher giving blood. May 2018 · Bulka Family Photo*

*Remembrance Day · Photo by Irving Osterer*

*Rabbi Bulka and Rabbi Scher on Canadian stamps*

*Playing with a grandchild · Bulka Family Photo*

*In his home library · Bulka Family Photo*

## *Chapter 9*

# A Family Man

"Family is not an important thing. It's everything."

*–Michael J. Fox*

Perhaps one of the lesser-known facets of logotherapy is the idea of discovering meaning through what we take from this world. There is perhaps no greater "take" on planet Earth than deriving *Nakhat* (pride) from one's children.

Rabbi Bulka's involvement in the Ottawa community may have precluded him from spending large quantities of time with his family, but there was never a shortage of quality.

Rabbi Bulka's oldest son, Shmuel Bulka, notes:

> "From a personal perspective I can say that this was most definitely not the case. Yes, we had some vacations cut short because my father ran back to Ottawa for a funeral, but at least on a personal level, I benefitted from my father's willingness to go anywhere and everywhere just to spend time with his kids. Growing up, we often went to hockey or baseball games in Montreal and many other places across North America. Even in more recent years, I had many opportunities to go to different places with my father, even if just for a few hours, spending time alone with him without distraction or interruption. A good way to sum it up would be to say that most of my father/son time with my father was very high quality, full of meaningful and memorable moments."

As one of Rabbi Bulka's grandchildren, here's where I can come in and share my own personal anecdote about Rabbi Bulka.

It was Sukkot 2011, and my family was traveling to Ottawa for the first part of the weeklong holiday.

My siblings, parents, and I looked forward to taking this yearly road trip (as we would always go to Ottawa for Sukkot), and were prepared with games, toys, and snacks.

Six hours into our trip, we finally arrived at the border. We used the opportunity to call my grandparents back in New York to let them know we were almost in Canada and about two hours away from my grandparents in Ottawa. In those days, we didn't have the ability to call and text between the U.S. and Canada, so this was the last time we would be speaking to them for some time.

Because other cousins would be in Ottawa for the holiday, we opted to stay at my father's close friend's home, around the corner from my grandparents.

My grandfather had left the key to the house we were staying at inside the house, near his front door. We had told my grandfather that since it was late, my father would slip into the house to grab the keys and then we would come back to my grandparents' house the next morning. We promptly headed to sleep after an extremely long car ride.

As we were heading into bed with the exhausting road trip behind us, my grandparents noticed the key's absence. They hadn't heard anyone slip in and immediately thought it might have gotten lost in the shuffle of moving furniture to accommodate the cousins who were staying over.

My grandfather decided to call our host to see if he could retrieve another key. Our host was in Israel, and Rabbi Bulka made many attempts to contact him before finally getting through. Our host told Rabbi Bulka that there was a spare key hidden in the garage. At around 4 AM, Rabbi Bulka drove over in hopes of returning with the extra key.

Meanwhile, our car was parked outside the garage, with a New York license plate and our signature "sensfan2" plates on our Toyota Sienna.

For some reason, my grandfather didn't notice the car, and started to panic that it was 4 AM and we hadn't yet arrived.

Rabbi Bulka called my father's phone furiously, but after six unsuccessful calls (we were sleeping!), he decided to take things to the next level. Rabbi Bulka always had a phenomenal relationship with the Ottawa Police; and he used his connections to get in touch with Border Control to find out if we had passed through.

Unfortunately, Rabbi Bulka gave the wrong license plate number (he was off by one number), and the Border Control expressed their apologies, but they had no record of our passing the border.

Rabbi Bulka himself drove out to Watertown, NY, the town right past the border from Canada to the U.S., to see if he could find car wreckage or a cliff that our car might have swerved on. When he couldn't find us, he assumed the worst and felt it was time to call my mother's parents in New York.

When my mother woke up the next morning, she called her parents to wish them a good holiday, and was met with sobs on the other end, almost as if she were back from the dead.

I remember that day well. My father recalls it as the only time in his life when my grandfather looked panicked. Prior to the start of the holiday meal that night, my grandfather, still visibly shaken, talked about how much his children and grandchildren meant to him.

* * *

Rabbi Bulka's oldest child, a daughter, Yocheved, was born in 1968, closely followed by my father, Shmuel, in 1969, and then another daughter, Rena, in 1970.

Looking back on the early years, Rabbi Bulka remembered: "My dear late Naomi was a super Mom, respected everywhere she went. Quiet dignity but never pushy or loud or anything."

Rabbi Bulka recalled the nagging question of his children's education in Ottawa. Most of the schools in Ottawa were not at the same level of Orthodoxy that the Bulka family practiced at home. Eventually, Rabbi Bulka and his wife, Naomi, made the difficult choice to send their daughters to school in Montreal.

At a certain point, Naomi began to feel as though she were missing some of her children's most formative years. She decided, together with Rabbi Bulka, to embark on a sabbatical for a year to Israel so that they could spend more time with all of their children. For my grandfather, this was difficult, as there were already events that had been booked in the shul. Rabbi Bulka parceled the shul events into sections and managed to keep his commitments while still being there with his family.

Yocheved Shonek, my aunt, recalls that year spent in Israel. She remembers that each *Rosh Chodesh* (the first day of the Hebrew month), her father took her out to eat in a nice restaurant because he said it was a special Jewish holiday for women and that his wife needed a break.

In true Rabbi Bulka fashion, he managed to balance parental strictness with a healthy dose of sweetness, namely "nosh." His children remember there was a place called "up there" with his hidden stash of sweets, and if they were deserving, they would get some.

His children also recall that any time they went on a trip, they would stop at a gas station to get some treats, and they remember their father spending lots of time asking the gas attendant about his life. His vocation gave him the potential to influence the world in ways that perhaps other people might not be able to. I believe, though, that regardless of vocation, my grandfather would say that it is still possible to make a "gigantic" difference. (As much as there were words my grandfather did not like, there were some he often used, and "gigantic" is a word that just screams "Sabba" to me.)

* * *

When I asked Rabbi Bulka's children, my father and aunts and uncles, to reminisce about their father, they all had a similar sentiment. Rabbi Bulka used each minute of his time thoughtfully, never one to waste or kill time (he detested the phrase "kill time"- "Why would you want to kill it?" he'd wonder, "It is so valuable!").

As an aside, I am currently editing this chapter in the airport. I am a planner by nature, but as soon as a uniformed woman took the microphone at our gate, I knew we were in for a delay. The first thought that crossed my mind was "two hours to kill." Then my grandfather's voice sounded in my mind; so, I set out to write and edit, imagining the many times my grandfather probably edited his own manuscripts in airport lounges. I felt connected to him in a whole new way.

Anyway, back to the script:

My father recalls that even when my grandfather was at a hockey game, on occasion between periods, he would take a few minutes to review his latest manuscript. In fact, my uncle recalls that there was always some kind of reading material sticking out of his back pocket at a game. "He wasn't much of a relaxer," his children recall. "But he still took great care of himself and exercised daily and was careful with what he ate."

Though Rabbi Bulka did not like to waste time, he certainly was not always working. As mentioned earlier, whenever any of his children or grandchildren gave birth, he would fly, or if necessary, drive in to see the new baby in the hospital. He spent a lot of time traveling, and there was no occasion that was unattainable in terms of being able to attend. If there were enough hours in the day to get there and back, Rabbi Bulka would be on the road.

Even when they were young, Rabbi Bulka went on trips with his children. In 1987, he took one of his children on a trip to Houston to see three baseball games. He took other kids for a few days in Los Angeles. They were short trips, but still represented quality time carved out for his family.

A special trip on which Rabbi Bulka's children had the privilege to accompany him was the trip he routinely made to Smith Falls, Ontario for a kosher supervision check at the Hershey plant. They would get up early in the morning, excited to embark on a long car ride with their father. They were able to walk on the ground floor where only the workers were allowed, and help Rabbi Bulka oversee the *kashering* process in the Hershey plant. In fact, they were able to participate in the process that would make famous choclates like "Oh Henry" kosher. Rabbi Bulka usually took one child at a time on this trip, and it was always a treat to be "chosen."

On one occasion, my father treated Rabbi Bulka to a Mets game with him and his son (Rabbi Bulka's grandson). Because Rabbi Bulka didn't pay for the tickets, he insisted on buying and paying for food. He asked my father if he wanted a beer. My father quickly replied "No," but then my grandfather proceeded to buy himself one. "Wait," my father thought. "I don't think I have ever seen my father drink a beer. A chance to have a beer with my father? Why not?"

Rabbi Bulka had the opportunity to learn with many of his grandchildren for their Bar Mitzvahs, and he taught my brother the Torah portion for his Bar Mitzvah. They learned together long distance (from Canada to the U.S.) long before the advent of Zoom. Even when my grandfather was on the road driving while listening to my brother read the Torah portion over the phone, he was able to correct him from a distance.

My father recalled one of the greatest moments of his life watching his son Avi reading his Torah portion and his father standing by Avi's side. My father said he thought he saw my grandfather wipe away a tear, a rare occurrence, as he stood up there with them.

Any time my grandfather visited his children or grandchildren, he always brought treats. If you ever told my grandfather there was something you liked, you would receive loads of it the next time he came to visit. Be it coconut, bread from a certain bakery, Arizona Iced Tea, or a specific kind of "nosh," Rabbi Bulka tracked it down and brought it with him in multitudes. When Rideau Bakery, the kosher bakery in Ottawa was closing, he called each of his children to ask everything they liked from Rideau so he could "clean them out". In fact, when I spoke to people in Ottawa, they told me the same thing. Rabbi Bulka would often bring friends in Ottawa treats they had requested from New York, and family in New York treats they had requested from Ottawa. He never stopped thinking about others.

As much as Rabbi Bulka tried to be all things to all people, his children did miss the opportunity to see him regularly, and they expected that in 2015, when he became Rabbi Emeritus, they would see a lot more of him. What they did not expect was that in those later years, my grandfather would further commit himself to the Ottawa community by purchasing the house that he had lived in for so many years (originally part of his salary for his Rabbinical position).

In truth, so many of the things that my grandfather achieved took place in those later years when he was Rabbi Emeritus because he had much more time to be involved in different organizations, leaving a lot of the day-to-day work to the new Rabbi, Rabbi Idan Scher.

While Rabbi Bulka's children were disappointed at the time that he didn't move out of Ottawa, the six months after Rabbi Bulka's diagnosis and the outpouring of love he received showed his children that he had truly been needed in the Ottawa community. His children understood that their father had used every minute meaningfully while he was active in the Ottawa community and that accomplishing his purpose in life required him to stay in Ottawa.

As soon as Rabbi Bulka was diagnosed, his mindset shifted. He understood that although his life's purpose did not change, his means of accomplishing his purpose shifted. He knew that he no longer had the capacity to give to the community in the same way, and he left Ottawa with a sense of calm, knowing that he had given his community everything he had.

When Rabbi Bulka arrived in New York in January of 2021, he continued to communicate with his congregation and others from around the world, albeit by email rather than in person. In fact, his primary focus in his first few days in New York was to read and respond to the 1,000s (no exaggeration) of emails he received, each with a personal message (and only typing with two fingers, as per usual).

For the six months Rabbi Bulka was in New York following his diagnosis, he was surrounded by family daily. His wife, Leah, was by his side constantly, and he received visits from his children and grandchildren throughout the day.

Personally, I found the last six months of his life to be a very special time. I had never lived close to my grandfather, and though through the most unfortunate of circumstances, the proximity we enjoyed for those months (we lived about a three-minute drive away from each other) was priceless. It afforded me the opportunity to visit often and create memories I never would have had otherwise.

I think many of Rabbi Bulka's children and grandchildren felt this way. Even the ones who did not live close by had the opportunity to spend quality time with Rabbi Bulka. My father and Aunt Yocheved, who both lived nearby, visited my grandfather virtually every day.

Despite living countries apart, there were some special privileges that my grandfather's children did get to enjoy when he lived in Ottawa. I personally remember going with my family to Ottawa during the Sukkot holiday and having a meeting set up the day before Sukkot for my family and Rabbi Bulka to meet with the Prime Minister of Canada. In fact, the picture of my family and PM Stephen Harper hangs in the front hallway of my parents' home. (Fun fact: Whenever my siblings or I brought home a date, my father would test him/her to see if he/she could identify the prime minister).

My grandfather tried diligently to follow whatever his father did but did not impose these stringencies on his children. Rabbi Bulka's own children lost their mother before Rabbi Bulka had lost any of his parents. Once Rabbi Bulka lost his parents, he fasted yearly to commemorate the day of his parents' death. My father had not adopted this custom when his mother passed away. In an ironic twist, Rabbi Bulka himself passed away on a communal fast day, so his children will be fasting on the day of his death for years to come, even without officially adopting it as a custom.

One of the main tenets of logotherapy is finding meaning in life through what you give to the world. One of the fundamental ways Rabbi Bulka did that is through his family. Not only did he invest in his relationships with each of his children, but all five of his children have inherited the traits of their father in some way or another, which has created another layer of meaning that traverses generations.

The opening passage of *Pirkay Avot*, which traces the transmission of Torah from generation to generation, sets the stage for a deeper understanding of the importance of imparting values and virtues. As it states, "Moshe received the Torah from Sinai and transmitted it to Yehoshua, and Yehoshua to the Elders, and the Elders to the Prophets, and the Prophets transmitted the Torah to the Men of the Great Assembly."[1] This emphasis on the transmission process highlights the significance of passing down not only knowledge but also positive character traits and ethical principles.

In the case of Rabbi Bulka, this tradition of transmission manifested in the remarkable qualities inherited by his children. Just as *Pirkay Avot* stresses the importance of transmitting integrity and wisdom, Rabbi Bulka instilled in his children a strong sense of compassion, kindness, and respect for others. They became the living embodiments of the values their father cherished and actively promoted.

Upon Rabbi Bulka's diagnosis, a close family friend from Ottawa, Dr. Harry Prizant, was in Israel and contacted Rabbi Bulka's youngest son who lives in Jerusalem: Rabbi Binyonim Bulka. Dr. Prizant wanted to know if there was anything that Binyomin wished to deliver to his father in Ottawa. Binyomin had some family photos he thought his father would enjoy and made plans with Dr. Prizant to meet on Shalom Aleichem Street to hand off the photographs. Binyomin arrived at the meeting place in Jerusalem with the pictures but didn't see Dr. Prizant there. It turned out that Dr. Prizant was referring to Shalom Aleichem Street in Tel Aviv, not Jerusalem, an hour-long bus ride away. Without missing a beat, Binyomin hopped on a bus to deliver the pictures. Once Binyomin made up his mind that the pictures would be meaningful to his father, in true Rabbi Bulka fashion, he went to whatever lengths necessary to get them into the right hands. To Binyomin, the obligation and opportunity to honor one's parents knows no bounds.

Rabbi Bulka's oldest daughter, Yocheved Shonek, rivals the time her own father spent visiting patients in the hospital. When Yocheved's sister-in-law had a sick child in a hospital in North Carolina, Yocheved went there frequently from her New York home to the point that the doctors trusted her as much as they trusted the patient's mother. It wasn't easy for Yocheved to leave her own large family behind, but

---

1. Pirkay Avot 1:1, (Bulka, Ktav, Publishing).

she flew down to North Carolina at the drop of a hat, and always anticipated the needs of the family from start to finish. Because of her experiences and her empathetic nature, Yocheved became a patient liaison for the organization, Chesed 24/7, which according to its website, provides "extensive and innovative services to the sick, the elderly, the developmentally disabled, and any individual or family facing a life challenge." Yocheved is a person who anticipates the needs of others and dedicates her life to her relationships and to caring for others, much like Rabbi Bulka himself.

My father, Shmuel Bulka, Rabbi Bulka's oldest son, inherited Rabbi Bulka's integrity. On one occasion when my father traveled to Israel, he purchased a burger from Burger Ranch at the airport. After the long flight, when my father checked his credit card statement, he noticed that he had not been charged for the burger. For many, this would have been a nice treat – it was the store's error – and he as the consumer could have benefitted. For my father, this wouldn't suffice. His niece was going to Israel the next week, and he asked her to go to Burger Ranch to explain the issue and pay for the burger, which she did.

Rena, my grandfather's daughter, embodies the trait of consistency and commitment that her father, my grandfather, so strongly believed in, especially when it comes to volunteerism. She and her family have quietly adopted various charitable causes and makes sure to consistently address their needs. For example, the Chesed 24/7 charity prepares tuna, crackers, and baby carrots every Sunday for those patients in need of meals. Rena is there consistently, every Sunday, preparing these care packages. This may seem like a small act, but it is a powerful reminder of the values and principles that my grandfather instilled in her: when you commit to something, you stick to it, especially when others are depending on you. Even during a busy or unpredictable life, Rena makes time to honor this commitment, knowing that someone is relying on her kindness.

Similarly, Eliezer, my grandfather's second-to-youngest son, has inherited my grandfather's linguistic precision and overall attention to detail. Like my grandfather, Eliezer understands the importance of being exact in the words you choose. My grandfather was known for his exceptional ability to correct someone reading the Torah, even over the phone, as my own brother found out when studying for his Bar Mitzvah. Eliezer has followed this example. Not only has he published a blog dedicated to the Hebrew laws of grammar, known as *Dikduk,* but Eliezer has been tasked as the only person in his synagogue who is allowed to correct someone for an incorrect pronunciation, not just because of his expertise, but because, like my grandfather, he knows how to do so in the proper manner so that the person being corrected does not feel bad. (I can attest to this as well, as Eliezer has been a phenomenal editor of this book- he did not hold back on making comments, and yet made them in the most palatable of ways.)

My grandfather was a model of virtue, embodying qualities such as selflessness, empathy, integrity, consistency, commitment, and precision in all aspects of his life. These traits were not only evident in his character, but, as evidenced above, also in the way he raised his children, instilling in them the same values that he held dear. Through his example, he taught them the importance of leading a life guided by purpose and meaning, a core tenet of logotherapy. His legacy continues to inspire and guide us to this day.

## LETTER #1: REFLECTIONS FROM A GRANDCHILD

Shortly before Sabba became sick, I was zocheh (merited) to start learning b'chavrusa (together) over the phone with him on a weekly basis. This was not our first time doing this; a few years before my bar mitzvah, we had begun Mishnayos Seder Nashim, hoping to complete it in time for the occasion (b'chasdei Hashem-with the kindness of God-we did, with plenty of time left).

It was around four years later when my Sabba began suggesting that we start learning together again. Whenever he'd bring it up, I'd push the idea to the back of my mind, until, eventually, I realized the value of the opportunity and accepted the offer, and we began learning Sefer HaChinuch (a book that goes through the 613 commandments in detail).

After Sabba's hospital stay, I wasn't sure when and if he would want to continue learning. Heeding my mother's advice, after a three-week pause, I called Sabba and asked if he would like to continue learning. He did, with the request, if I wouldn't mind, to do the reading, which I was more than happy to do. Despite Sabba's weak voice, he continued to stimulate me with his thought-provoking questions and his novel and profound insights into the words of the Chinuch.

Eventually, Sabba became too weak to continue our learning, and we left off in middle of Mitzva (commandment) 16, the commandment to not break a bone from the Korban Pesach. I was quite distraught with the thought that we'd stopped in middle of a Mitzva, and that, with the way Sabba's condition was deteriorating, it didn't seem likely that we'd learn again.

Motza'ei Shabbos (Saturday night), the night before Shiva Asar B'Sammuz (hebrew date, Jewish fast day), my mother sadly informed me that the time had come to "say goodbye to Sabba". Though this news was very difficult to accept, denying reality was something Sabba would not stand for.

That night, I was zocheh (merited) to have a few minutes with Sabba, and, although he wasn't conversing verbally, he nodded in response to my questions. On a whim, I decided to take out the Sefer HaChinuch, and I began reading aloud from where we had left off in Mitzva 16. The Chinuch was in middle of his famous response to the "foolish" question of the seeming superfluousness of the numerous mitzvos commemorating yetzias mitzrayim (exodus from Egypt), where he explains how a person's external actions impact his psyche, and he ends off explaining to the reader that his life's mission is to follow the Torah's Mitzvos (commandments) and not veer from them even briefly, lest his "quick" actions impact him to veer further.

It was with these words of the Chinuch, which Sabba so embodied-always thinking before acting and making sure that what he was doing was what he felt Hashem wanted, that I said my goodbye to him.

# Chapter 10
# Turning Grief Into Gratitude

> "Love goes very far beyond the physical person of the beloved. It finds its deepest meaning in his spiritual being, his inner self. Whether or not he is actually present, whether or not he is still alive at all, ceases somehow to be of importance."
>
> – *Viktor E. Frankl*

Rabbi Bulka was there for everyone in their times of sorrow, but what about his own life?

Rabbi Bulka and his wife, Naomi, after many pregnancy losses, suffered the terrible tragedy of the loss of their two-month-old son nine years into their marriage.

Unfortunately, in her early fifties, my grandmother, Naomi, was diagnosed with breast cancer. When she was first diagnosed, they were given an optimistic prognosis. In fact, my grandfather recalled the oncologist saying, "Don't worry, I'm going to cure your wife." That worried my grandfather as he did not trust that someone could have such certainty that he would be able to cure someone. That certainty, according to my grandfather, was reserved only for God.

My grandmother went into remission for a few years only to find out later that the cancer had spread. She went through chemotherapy treatments, but unfortunately, they were not doing the trick.

There was a stem cell transplant trial being conducted in Maryland at the time, and my grandmother's younger sister, Hunnie, graciously donated stem cells for the cause.

Unfortunately, my grandmother's immune system was at zero, and her organs had shut down before the procedure was able to prove helpful.

It was a difficult time for Rabbi Bulka and his children, but the saving grace for his children was that they still had their father. Following my grandmother's death, Rabbi Bulka took care of all the details, finances, and decision-making so the children could focus on grieving the loss of such a wonderful woman.

I was only five years old when my grandmother passed away, but I remember glimpses of her. Her delicious challah, sledding in the streets of Ottawa during the winter.

My grandmother was reserved and dignified, quiet and unassuming. She was also extremely determined. After she had all her children, she went back to college in order to get a computer science degree. She became a technical writer for Nortel, she helped people find their soulmate, and developed a remarkable identity that far surpassed just being a "Rabbi's wife." Her determination led her to remarkable achievements, including the opportunity to speak at a symposium on Women and Judaism. During her lecture, she shared valuable insights on balancing her roles as a Rebbetzin (Rabbi's wife) and a professional working for a high-tech company.

> She had a keen intellect that she used to pursue education and professional life at Nortel. She had a clear sense of duty as a wife, mother, daughter, sister, Rebbetzin and volunteer. She completed her husband. She dotted his i's and crossed his t's literally and figuratively…
>
> Thirty-four years ago, a very different community embraced a newlywed couple who gave up much to build a new life in Ottawa. Thirty-four years later, that same couple is largely responsible for this community being the vibrant active Jewish center it is…
>
> And though Reuven Bulka, the Rabbi, the professional, the advocate, the celebrity, the athlete, is front and centre, it was Naomi, the Rabbi's wife, the professional's wife, the advocate's wife and yes, the celebrity and the athlete's wife, who gave him

> the support, the encouragement, the strength, and the freedom to be all those things.[2]

Her death was obviously very difficult for my grandfather as he was now a widower in his fifties, with much life ahead of him. Once again, he sunk himself into his work and eventually wrote a book entitled *Grieving: Personal Reflections* following his wife's death. He also established a center for families who were dealing with a loved one battling cancer in Ottawa. Eventually, Rabbi Bulka wrote *Turning Grief into Gratitude*, which included reflections on mourning from the experience of losing his son, wife, and parents. Regarding his wife's death, Rabbi Bulka wrote:

> When Naomi passed away, it seemed like the world of our family had collapsed. The intensity of love that my children shared with her was matched by the intensity of the grief they felt at her passing. I am sure that, at the time, I cried as much for my children as I did for the loss I felt for my life-partner.[3]

She passed away on May 18, 2001, just before Shabbat in Washington and the funeral service took place on the following Sunday at Machzikei Hadas in Ottawa. Rabbi Bulka was especially filled with sorrow for his youngest son, who would have to stand under the Chuppah without his mother.

Within that year, Rabbi Bulka was introduced to Leah Kalish, a widow herself. After a few meetings, Rabbi Bulka and Leah decided to get married and start the next chapter of their lives together.

Leah is and always has been a part of the family. When she married my grandfather, she had two single sons: Chuli and Sariel. Over the years, we have enjoyed celebrating with them at both of their weddings and the births of many of their children. They were always like children and grandchildren to Rabbi Bulka, and by extension, they were family to Rabbi Bulka's family.

---

2. *Ottawa Jewish Bulletin*, June 18, 2001.
3. Bulka, Reuven P., *Turning Grief Into Gratitude*, (Ottawa, Canada: Paper Spider, 2007), 83.

About four years into their new marriage, Rabbi Bulka and Leah suffered the loss of their own parents.

My grandfather details the death of his parents in depth in his book *Turning Grief into Gratitude*. As I read through his thoughts, feelings, and actions surrounding his own parents' death, it instantly reminded me of my father and his siblings' thoughts, feelings, and actions surrounding my grandfather's death.

My grandfather's father was sick for some time and living in Israel while my grandfather resided in Ottawa. His sister, Rebecca, often went to Israel to check in on their parents. On the day my great-grandfather passed away, my grandfather wrote:

> There was no time to sit down and cry, because from the moment we found out, around 6:30 in the morning Jerusalem time, we were pressed into action to ensure that the funeral would take place that day. That is the Jewish way, to drop everything and to focus exclusively on attending to the deceased and making all the necessary arrangements.[4]

As an aside, this reminded me a lot of the way my father and his siblings reacted to my grandfather's death. He passed away early Sunday morning on a Jewish fast day, the 17th of Tammuz, and his children immediately made plans to ensure that the funeral would take place later that same day.

Even during my great-grandfather's *shiva* (7-day mourning period), my great-grandmother's health was in decline. My grandfather had returned to Israel for my great-grandfather's memorial ceremony, which took place 30 days after his death.

As my grandfather wrote, "The day after the memorial for my father, I flew to New York on my return trip to Ottawa for the Sabbath. I was very much aware of the life hanging in the balance, but Mom, in her quiet way, was quite tenacious, strong of heart, refusing to surrender".[5]

---

4. Ibid., 21.
5. Ibid., 23.

Almost as soon as my grandfather landed in New York, he was told by his sister that it was a matter of hours and was urged to return. "Thankfully," my grandfather wrote, "I was able to get a return flight to Israel almost immediately, which got me there by early Friday morning. When I landed, I learned that Mom had passed away while I was in flight".[6] My grandfather reflected about his parents' death in great detail in his aforementioned book. He writes that there was a "tension between sadness at the passing of my dear father and a gratitude for having my father for the major part of my life".[7]

Like everything in life, my grandfather harnessed a difficult moment and channeled it for positivity. He took his grief and transformed it into gratitude.

"Everything can be taken from a man but one thing: the last of the human freedoms- to choose one's attitude in any given set of circumstances, to choose one's own way".[8]

The words from Pirkay Avot, "All is foreseen yet freedom [of choice] is given,"[9] further underscore the importance of personal agency. While the future may be uncertain and certain events may be predetermined, each individual possesses the freedom to shape their own path through the choices they make. In the face of adversity, my grandfather demonstrated the remarkable power of gratitude. He refused to let grief consume him but instead transformed it into a profound appreciation for life's blessings. Through this shift in perspective, he embraced the freedom to choose his own way, refusing to be defined or limited by circumstances.

In fact, Rabbi Bulka even used his own suffering and grief as an opportunity to teach others what to say to someone in the throes of mourning, as there is a whole chapter at the end of his book dedicated to "what not to say to a mourner." My grandfather always found meaning in difficulty, and his parents' death was no exception.

6. Ibid.
7. Ibid., 85.
8. Frankl, *Man's Search for Meaning*, 61.
9. Pirkay Avot 3:15, (Bulka, Ktav Publishing).

## LETTER #1

One Thursday morning at 2 AM, I got a phone call from someone in the hospital saying that his wife is very sick, looking for Rabbi Bulka. Rabbi Bulka was away with his wife for the first time. While he was still away, word had come to Rabbi Bulka that the woman had died. This woman was a star pupil that attended his weekly classes. Rabbi Bulka left his holiday in Virginia Beach, drove his wife to New York, flew to Ottawa, and did the funeral on Friday morning. Then, he came after the funeral to be menachem avel (comfort the mourners) and flew back to New York because there was a kiddush for the naming of a baby in his family. He flew back to Ottawa later that day, and got there about five minutes before Shabbos started. He gave up his first holiday with his wife, and almost missed a family kiddush to be kind to his constituents.

## LETTER #2

When I was 10 years old my father died very suddenly of a heart attack. My mother instinctively called Rabbi Bulka to come to our house to help at the same time she called the paramedics. I don't remember much (I believe it is because it was so traumatic), but I vividly remember Rabbi Bulka reaching out his hand to me when I was standing in my living room. It was evening, I was only in my little nightgown. The paramedics had my father lying on the ground preparing to attempt CPR. I grabbed Rabbi Bulka's hand and had to step over my father's body to move out of the way to another room. I was in fact stepping over a threshold into a new life without my father. It was Rabbi Bulka's hand outstretched which helped me over this threshold. A kind Jewish hand helping me. It was the beginning of my long road to healing. It was his hand that began this journey for me. I am forever grateful and wish he knew I am thinking of him and care for him deeply.

# *Chapter 11*
# A Citizen of Ottawa

> "Rabbi Bulka would also bring treats when he came in to do his Sunday night show. Candy, chocolate, and one time he brought in cookies n' cream ice cream cones. He had a signature high five following the show as well. RIP Rabbi."
>
> – *Stephen Bunda, TSN 1200 (The Ottawa radio station)*

One of the blessings of Rabbi Bulka's congregation was their deep appreciation for Rabbi Bulka's involvement outside the shul with the community at large. The shul easily could have requested that Rabbi Bulka concentrate solely on his role as Rabbi, but they appreciated the community's exposure to their Rabbinic leader, and at the same time, it helped to expand the shul's profile. Because Ottawa is the capital city, there was a lot more opportunity for involvement in the media.

A sure way to become known in the community is to be on television. Rabbi Bulka had a colleague in Toronto who asked him if he'd be interested in taking over the show he had at that time, *Facets in Good Faith*. The show featured a rotation of religious leaders as hosts, many of whom had dropped out over time. Rabbi Bulka found himself doing many of the shows and was careful not to make it "too Jewish," as he wanted all people to be able to relate to them. Rabbi Bulka attempted and succeeded in making the program meaningful and universal across all faiths, and even to those with no faith at all.

Radio was another medium through which Rabbi Bulka became well known. Rabbi Bulka became good friends with Dennis Prager of

Los Angeles, the current host of *The Dennis Prager Show*, and one of America's most well-known radio talk show hosts. Prager invited Rabbi Bulka to be his guest on a Sunday. Prager refused to allow Rabbi Bulka any time for preparation, and he instead was given a topic on the spot to discuss for two hours on Sunday night during a segment entitled "Religion on the Line." At the time, Prager was local, but Rabbi Bulka predicted he would become a "somebody."

Rabbi Bulka recalled Prager's funny, brilliant, and articulate nature. Prager would choose an abstract topic and was able to go on about it for two hours.

Rabbi Bulka decided that if this could be done in L.A., why not Ottawa? Rabbi Bulka called the local radio station and asked if they would like a program modeled after Dennis Prager's "Religion on the Line." They agreed and gave him the 10 PM slot on Sunday night, a time when almost no one is listening to the radio. Rabbi Bulka went with it, and it started to take off. A couple of years in, he was asked to do the show for two-hour segments, so he started doing the show from 9–11 every Sunday night. Eventually, it became known as "Sunday Night with Rabbi Bulka."

As a Rabbi, Sunday night was a prime evening for weddings, so Rabbi Bulka would often attend a wedding, leave within 20 minutes to nine, and go back to the wedding when the show ended at 11 PM.

He was so focused on the job that he didn't let anything distract him. On one occasion, when his daughter, Yocheved, gave birth to a baby in New York, my father, Shmuel Bulka, called the radio station as a caller to let his father know. The topic that night was alcoholism, and my father attempted to speak in code, incorporating the topic to tell his father about the new addition to the family. He asked: "If you are a recovering alcoholic and something happy happens like a sister giving birth, is it ok to celebrate with non-alcoholic beer?". Rabbi Bulka was so focused on the show that he didn't recognize his own son's voice, and he did not manage to decode the message at the time. My father eventually requested to speak to Rabbi Bulka during the break to finally share the news!

The final piece of media that expanded Rabbi Bulka's renown

throughout Ottawa was his contributions to *The Ottawa Citizen.* There was a weekly column called "Ask the Religion Experts," where a question was posed and leaders of different faiths answered the question. Rabbi Bulka represented the Jewish response for 15 years, from 1999 to 2014. There are a few books that he compiled that have all his answers in one place, and, through the generous permission of *The Ottawa Citizen,* I have included several that I thought were poignant at the end of this chapter.

As an expansion of his writing and his doctoral thesis which married psychology and Judaism, Rabbi Bulka also started an academic journal called *The Journal of Psychology and Judaism.* "We would have yearly conferences on psychology and Judaism in Los Angeles, and we would cover a wide variety of topics." During the first years of its existence, the journal had about 1000 subscribers. It began as an in-house operation; Rabbi Bulka's wife, Naomi, helped with it, too. It came out semi-annually, which gave the contributors plenty of time to get articles written and approved. Eventually, they sold it to Human Sciences Press, which began funding the publication. Unfortunately, they started charging subscribers such an exorbitant amount that readership of the journal began to dwindle.

Undoubtedly, Rabbi Bulka recognized the significance of writing, speaking, and engaging with a broad audience as a means to amplify the meaningfulness of his life. It is worth highlighting that he never pursued fame or notoriety; instead, he remained focused on his mission. As aptly conveyed in *Pirkay Avot,* "One who seeks a name, loses a name."[1] Frankl also echoed this sentiment, stating: "Man is originally characterized by his 'search for meaning' rather than his 'search for himself.' The more he forgets himself – giving himself to a cause or another person – the more *human* he is. And the more he is immersed and absorbed in something or someone other than himself the more he really becomes *himself*"[2]

1. Pirkay Avot 1:13, (Bulka, Ktav Publishing).
2. Frankl, Viktor E., *Man's Search for Ultimate Meaning.* (New York: Perseus Publishing, 2000), 91. Kindle.

Rabbi Bulka's dedication to a purpose greater than himself not only brought him fulfillment but also allowed him to leave a profound impact on those he served. Because of his deep impact on the Ottawa community, Rabbi Bulka was awarded with the keys to the City of Ottawa in February of 2010, an event that children (and some grandchildren) from abroad came to experience. Through becoming more involved as a citizen of Ottawa, Rabbi Bulka truly became himself and started to embody his "moniker" of "Canada's Rabbi."

## Chapter 11 – Excerpts and Letters

### *THE OTTAWA CITIZEN* – MARCH 23, 2014[3]

Ask the Religion Experts: What, if anything, has shaken your faith the most?

True, authentic faith is by definition unconditional. It would be a sorry state if every time something untoward occurred, that the believer would lose faith. If that happened, faith could hardly survive, since no one can go through a full life without battle scars. Very often, it is the unconditional faith that carries us through the trying, and yes, even the tragic times.

At the same time, there are certain realities in life that are shattering, that defy logic, that elicit a primal scream, that make you wonder – "why?" Why is this happening? Why is God allowing this to happen?

Verily, no painful situation should ever be dismissed away without being bothered by it. The prophets of old, surely true believers, still felt strongly enough about injustices in the world that they cried out to God. It was a cry from the heart, even though in their logical thinking, they knew that God had reasons that were beyond human comprehension.

Particularly devastating is a walk through the cancer ward at a Children's Hospital. Seeing children suffer, sometimes from birth, defies explanation. It is rattling. You have to be less than human not to wonder how this fits into God's game plan.

---

3. "Ask the Religion Experts," *The Ottawa Citizen*, March 23, 2014.

Events of history, the extent of the cruelty which so-called human beings have exhibited, are another rattler. Millions upon millions of people have been murdered by other people, surely poor excuses for human beings, but two-legged creatures nevertheless. Included in the millions are children and adults who have literally been butchered to death by criminals who were obviously undeterred by the cries of pain and agony, and sometimes even encouraged by the cries. How can one not be shaken by all this?

But being shaken is not the same as having one's faith shaken. And questioning why is not the same as having one's faith shaken. Thinking that we know the ways of God is a delusion at the best of times, but unconditional faith means that the faith is not compromised by the senseless and the evil. When we ask "why," there is no expected answer. It is a cry of pain, in faith.

Many things shake me, but my faith is unshaken. Without faith, it is almost impossible to arise from the shake.

## FEBRUARY 26, 2014[4]

Ask the Religion Experts: Does God have a sense of humour?

For openers, no one knows the definitive answer to this. We do not know God's ways, and ascribing to God human characteristics does God, or the concept of God, no favour. So, what follows herein would fall under the heading of anthropomorphic speculation, with all its inherent limitations.

Moving on from that significant caveat, I would not be surprised if what passes for humour, of the Leno, Letterman, O'Brien, or Kimmel variety, or whoever, may not elicit laughter from God.

This does not diminish the importance of laughter in our lives. Laughter has so many important benefits, including lowering the blood pressure (for everyone but the comic), offering a sense of perspective, energizing those with depleted batteries, and just plain making people feel good, even if only fleetingly.

---

4. "Ask the Religion Experts," *The Ottawa Citizen*, February 26, 2014

But all the reasons why humour is helpful to us mortals would not apply to God, for Whom high blood pressure is hardly an issue, Who hardly lacks for perspective, and certainly does not have depletable batteries.

I suspect that in asking your question, which is not as crazy as it sounds, you did not have crass humour in mind. Serious, life related humour, very often in the form of irony, leaving God "smiling," is more than a possibility.

We have the classic Talmudic story of sages who refused to allow a heavenly voice to dictate a matter of law, with the argument that once God gave the Torah, God's teaching, to the people, it belonged to them and God could no longer intervene.

The Talmud reports that God's reaction to this was not to be angry, but rather to smilingly concede that the sages were correct, that they had "triumphed" over God. If this turning of the tables on God does not exhibit a profound sense of humour, I do not know what would.

The most important takeaway from this is that it reinforces the interactive nature of our relation with God, that our actions resonate with God. That, funnily enough, is quite a serious and important matter.

## LETTER #1

We each have our own relationship and story with and about you cemented in our memories. They all make us smile and what is shared amongst us is your genuine interest, guidance, support, teachings, humour and countless kindnesses.

For me personally, I will always be grateful to you for interviewing me about Cyber Counseling on your radio show. Emes, that was way too much fun!! Gotta love CFRA with Rav Bulka 👍.

Ironic, how you have devoted much of your profession guiding others on how to navigate life challenges juxtaposed to now, you're facing the ultimate challenge possible.

With the strength and support of your family and community may you find peace and resolve in a life lived fully beyond measure.

## LETTER #2

Dear Rabbi Bulka. I don't think I ever told you how much your visits meant to me while I was recuperating from a near fatal car accident that occurred in December 2007. I knew you from working at CFRA. Of course, everybody knew you, and you were friendly and warm to everyone, pulling candies out of your pockets and treating us to delicious cakes whenever there was a celebration. But when you showed up at my bedside one afternoon at the Civic Hospital, I have to admit I was surprised to see you. However, I shouldn't have been, because I knew you were a kind, caring and giving individual. So me in the bed with a broken back and broken hip, you sitting in the chair next to me, and we're chatting away like old friends. And it wasn't just the one time either. You came back again. and always lifted my spirits. I wanted to let you know I will never forget that, Rabbi Bulka, and I pray you find comfort and strength for this journey you are now on.

*Chapter 12*

# A Rabbi's Rabbi

> "Leadership is about making others better as a result of your presence and making sure that impact lasts in your absence."
>
> – *Rabbi Lord Jonathan Sacks*

If there was a single *sefer* (Jewish book) that benefited the Rabbinate more than any other, it would be *The* RCA *Life-Cycle Madrikh*, known as the lifecycle handbook for any Rabbi. According to one of Rabbi Bulka's Rabbinical colleagues, it is "a little book that is hands down the most important book for a Rabbi to have." There is rarely a Rabbinical library that does not include this sefer, and it is even given out to many Rabbis when they receive their *semichah* (Rabbinic ordination). The work goes through every life cycle event you can imagine with detailed instructions on how to officiate at each one.

Rabbi Bulka is the one who authored and compiled this extremely important *sefer*. In some ways, he accompanies everyone on every Jewish life cycle journey through his incredibly precise instructions written out in the *Life-cycle Madrikh*.

In fact, throughout the week of *shiva*, any Rabbi who came to pay a visit immediately brought up the *Life-cycle Madrikh*. "I just used it last night to perform a wedding," one Rabbi remarked.

This *Life-cycle Madrikh* is likely one of the essential contributing factors to Rabbi Bulka's title as a "Rabbi's Rabbi."

Perhaps nothing illustrates this title better than Rabbi Bulka's incredible relationship with his successor, Rabbi Idan Scher.

In 2015, Rabbi Bulka stepped down as the main Rabbi of Machzikei Hadas in order to allow a younger Rabbi to reinvigorate the shul and a new generation of congregants. Rabbi Bulka became the Rabbi Emeritus of Machzikei Hadas, and with that transition, he had less daily responsibility to the shul. Rabbi Idan Scher and his wife, Shifra, moved to Ottawa, first in the position of Associate Rabbi, and a year later becoming the Rabbi and Rebbetzin.

As Rabbi Bulka's family, we all expected this would result in more time spent in the States, more specifically New York, where Rabbi Bulka and his wife, Leah, owned a small apartment.

We also imagined that in order for the new Rabbi to grow into his position, Rabbi Bulka would have to take a step back.

We were amazed to see the unique bond that existed between Rabbi Bulka and Rabbi Scher, one that is not commonly found between a Rabbi and his successor. Both Rabbi Bulka and Rabbi Scher's incredible humility and respect for one another gave way to a special relationship from which the entire congregation benefited.

Rabbi Scher recounted the interview process when he came to Ottawa to apply for the position. He and his wife, Shifra, were invited into Rabbi Bulka's house, expecting to have a formal meeting. They were pleasantly surprised to enter the laid-back atmosphere that Rabbi Bulka had created for them in his living room.

Rabbi Bulka did not wear a jacket, his tie was undone, and his feet were up. He made Rabbi Scher and his wife feel extremely comfortable for an interview that would obviously be wrought with nerves for them.

Rabbi Scher was grateful for the relationship and mutual respect that he and my grandfather shared. It was one of deep reverence, yet at the same time, profound friendship.

For Rabbi Scher's 30th birthday, Rabbi Bulka gave him a beer mug with one of his signature beer puns. In fact, whenever Rabbi Bulka was in Montreal, he always thought of Rabbi Scher and his wife and brought them back the shawarma that he knew they enjoyed.

Generally, a new Rabbi wants to forge his own path, and a Rabbi Emeritus wants to continue to do things in his own way. There is often tension and friction between them, and this friction can trickle down to the congregation.

The dynamic between Rabbi Bulka and Rabbi Scher transcended any potential obstacles or differences. The relationship they fostered was characterized by mutual respect and a genuine support for one another. Rather than imposing his own methods or expecting conformity, Rabbi Bulka exemplified the essence of *Pirkay Avot's* wisdom: "Let your friend's honor be as dear to you as your own."[1] This verse encapsulates the profound value Rabbi Bulka placed on honoring and cherishing others, and allowing them to forge their own path forward.

Rabbi Scher shared that Rabbi Bulka became like a father and grandfatherly figure to him and his family, and that Rabbi Bulka was his biggest cheerleader in the Ottawa community. "Who wouldn't feel confident when they had the biggest cheerleader in Ottawa on their side?" Rabbi Scher remarked.

Through Rabbi Bulka's embodiment of the teachings of Pirkay Avot, he demonstrated the profound impact that can be achieved when individuals uplift and value one another. This beautiful example serves as a testament to the transformative power of cultivating relationships founded on mutual respect and the celebration of each other's unique qualities.

One piece of wisdom that Rabbi Bulka shared with Rabbi Scher was that there would be nothing more important for his success as a Rabbi than the way he showed up for people during important moments in their lives: when they are sick, near death, mourning or celebrating. One of the few actions Rabbi Bulka encouraged was for Rabbi Scher to frequent the Ottawa hospitals, which undoubtedly has had a positive impact on community members.

Rabbi Bulka was a trailblazer, unafraid to take on challenges that most shy away from. He advocated for all of the Jewish people, regardless of degree or level of observance. As a Rabbi, it is easy to be strict, but saying "no" doesn't require the same wisdom as saying "yes" and justifying your response.

---

1. Pirkay Avot 2:10, (Bulka, Ktav Publishing).

Rabbi Bulka was always ahead of his time, making sure the women in his congregation felt comfortable and part of the shul experience. He immediately intuited his own shul's needs and created a *mechitza* (the barrier wall between the men and women's section) that followed *halachic* (Jewish law) standards but still included the women in the prayer service. Over the years, my grandfather received a lot of pushback over the *mechitza*, but he was firm on his stance, confident in both the Jewish law behind it and the needs of his congregation.

Rabbi Bulka was a Rabbi's Rabbi, but with a tremendous sense of humility.

On one occasion, when Rabbi Bulka had his wallet out, a fellow saw a picture of a stately man who looked like he could be Rabbi Bulka's father.

"Was your father also a Rabbi?" the man asked.

"No," said Rabbi Bulka. "My father was a Rabbi. I am also a Rabbi."

As much as my grandfather loved his semantics and plays on words, this statement meant something deeper. Rabbi Bulka, though he is regarded as one of the most prominent Rabbis of our time, never felt like he came anywhere close to his father's level of greatness.

Over the period of his illness and following his death, Rabbi Bulka and his family received countless emails and messages from other Rabbis whom he inspired and mentored over the years.

Rabbi Bulka's influence is exponential, as it is forever multiplied by the number of people he inspired who then inspired others.

These sentiments have been a part and parcel of Rabbi Bulka's life and his propensity towards logotherapy. Upon reflecting on logotherapy and his relationship with Viktor Frankl, Rabbi Bulka explained that logotherapy is about finding meaning and purpose in life, and that it is something that can guide you through a host of problems. The trick, according to Rabbi Bulka, was that "it's not about me, but the world out there." Rabbi Bulka explained: "The more you go beyond yourself to embrace different issues and causes, the more you'll be better yourself. Some major problems we face in modern civilization is a focus on 'I, I, I.' You don't get anywhere if all you focus on is you and your own importance."

Rabbi Bulka's tenure in the Rabbinate fostered his constant focus on others above himself. Rabbi Bulka didn't let it stop with his own congregation; he ensured that future congregations and shuls around the world would benefit from his experiences and wisdom.

## Chapter 12 – Letters

### LETTER #1: RABBI EMERITUS, TEMPLE ISRAEL

You have been a monumental role model and a colleague whose wisdom I valued. Whatever HaShem has in store for us I know he brought me to Ottawa in order for me to learn the meaning of the word Rabbi from you.

### LETTER #2: RABBI OF OTTAWA TORAH CENTRE CHABAD

Since my first days in Ottawa 25 years ago you have been a role model for me as to what a askon tziburi and a Rov is really about. I have learned much from you and what you have done in this city is exemplary.

### LETTER #3: RABBI OF CONGREGATION BETH ORA IN MONTREAL

Finding myself somewhat isolated as a new Rabbi in Montreal, I left a voice message for the famous Rabbi Bulka at his synagogue. When Rabbi Bulka called me back I was struck by his warmth, by how down to earth he was, and by his interest in me as a person. Despite being a busy person with connections to many, he made time to see me before a lecture he gave in a different community. When I was seeking his advice a few months later, he actually came to Montreal specially to see me. Rabbi Bulka has always been available, accessible, down to earth, and a paragon of virtue. He is a friend, mentor and role model.

*Chapter 13*

# Not So Random Acts of Kindness

> "Throughout Canada, in each and every year, the third week of February is to be known as 'Kindness Week.'"
>
> – *The Honourable Senator Jim Munson, Bill S-223*

In 2008, Rabbi Bulka approached The United Way of Ottawa with a dream that he intended to bring to fruition. That dream? Kindness Week. A city-wide, weeklong event to engage the minds and hearts of Ottawans with kindness and generosity. The hope was that after spending a week immersing oneself in kind acts, it would encourage kindness beyond that week.

The first Kindness Week was pulled together in around a month's time, ready for the third week in February, which coincided with Valentine's day. The United Way, led by Jeff Turner, and Rabbi Bulka enlisted the help of a wide range of community leaders. Close to twenty people came on board, rallying behind Rabbi Bulka and this idea as they saw the value in creating this week of kindness.

Kindness Week produced a broad range of representation around the city. Notably, the schools took a liking to it and gradually set up Kindness Week in schools to target the fourth grade. The police chief as well as many other community leaders would speak to the students. And of course, Rabbi Bulka.

From the second year and onwards, Rabbi Bulka had to be chauffeured around the city as there was so much demand for him to personally attend all of the schools' presentations.

The event was launched at one of the downtown malls, and hundreds of people were in attendance. It became significant and people began looking forward to it each year.

Throughout the week, the many community leaders would involve themselves in acts of kindness. Police officers around Ottawa would pull over drivers in their cars or pedestrians on the road, and instead of handing them a speeding ticket, they created simulated tickets that read, "You were caught being kind." Typically, a close encounter with a police officer is intimidating and nerve-racking, but this kindness "gimmick" was something everyone enjoyed.

It was extremely important to Rabbi Bulka that Kindness Week be an interfaith event. Leaders from the Church, Imams, and other Rabbis participated in Kindness Week as well. They spoke to their congregations the week before in order to foster excitement for the event.

Rabbi Bulka was known for always carrying treats for people. His friend remarked that "his trunk seemed to be a grocery store." As such, the team decided to go to the airport during Kindness Week and welcome inbound passengers into Ottawa. Rabbi Bulka, together with Archbishop Terrence Prendergast of the Ottawa Diocese and Imam Samy Metwally handed out candies to each passenger as he/she stepped off the plane.

One year, they gave out Hershey's kisses. Unabashedly, Rabbi Bulka went up to total strangers walking off the plane and exclaimed, "It's Kindness Week in Ottawa. Would you like a kiss?" The next year, he added Hershey's hugs to the mix. In one of the last years of Rabbi Bulka's life, they greeted refugees, too, who were arriving at the airport during Kindness Week.

Even just as Kindness Week in Ottawa was starting to take off, Rabbi Bulka couldn't help but think bigger. A few years later, the concept was adopted on a provincial level (across Ontario). Rabbi Bulka imagined Kindness Week on a national scale. He was planting the seeds for a National Kindness Week in Canada.

Jeff Turner, the former National Director of the United Way Centraide Canada in Ottawa, and a close friend of Rabbi Bulka, lobbied with Rabbi Bulka in the Senate in an effort to nationalize Kindness Week. It took around two years to get the legislation written. Jeff Turner and Rabbi Bulka sat with Senator Jim Monson in front of a senate hearing and answered all the questions that came their way.

The bill was read once, but before the second reading, the session of Parliament ended, and the bill was shut down.

Recently, the bill was reintroduced and the text of the legislation was updated.

On June 3, 2021, mere weeks before his passing, Rabbi Bulka's dream became a reality, when the Honourable Senator Munson officially declared in Bill S-223, "Throughout Canada, in each and every year, the third week of February is to be known as Kindness Week."

Concurrently, Rabbi Bulka began working on a new endeavor called "Kind Canada Genereux." It is clear to anyone who has been to Canada that Canadians are naturally kind. In fact, people often make fun of Canadians for the number of times they utter "sorry," even when something doesn't warrant an apology. Rabbi Bulka wanted to make Canada the kindest country in the world, and he sought to create an organization that would further that cause.

Ron Prehogan, a long-time friend and colleague of Rabbi Bulka, sat on the board as the organization's vice president at its inception. Kind Canada Generoux introduced many initiatives over the course of its fewer than 10-year existence. Notably, it created a Kindness curriculum in high schools in response to bullying and gave out Kindness cards to employees. Rabbi Bulka eventually transferred the reins of the organization to Ron Prehogan, who has amazing ideas that will hopefully continue the Kind Canada legacy and continue to bring Rabbi Bulka's ideas and dreams to life.

When I asked my grandfather a little bit more about kindness and his desire to make kindness week happen throughout Canada, he told me about his disdain for the idea of "random kindness." Rabbi Bulka believed that kindness shouldn't be random, but instead, it should be purposeful, and it should be bountiful.

Rabbi Bulka felt that kind people always rose to the fore. It was for this reason that he wanted to get fellow Candians to devote a few seconds a day thinking about what they could do to make someone else's day.

My grandfather told me a story that is likely just one of many similar situations in which he found himself. He was in a bookstore making a purchase and began to converse with the woman at the cash register. The woman began baring her soul to my grandfather and was clearly feeling very down. My grandfather said he listened very carefully to everything she said. Later on, she got his address and wrote my grandfather a thank you card.

My grandfather remarked: "How difficult is it to say a kind word to someone? It is uplifting, easy, and inexpensive. Kind words penetrate, as do unkind words. Saying good things are so much easier and the reward is so much more fulfilling. And it opens the door to the obvious- making the world a better place."

Clearly, Rabbi Bulka was fulfilling one of the three principal tenets of logotherapy: discovering meaning in what he gave to the world. In this case, it was the way he connected with others and in the way he tried to get others to connect with the world. He truly exemplified the teachings of *Pirkay Avot,* which encourages individuals to "Be of the disciples of Aharon – loving peace and pursuing peace"[1] and to exhibit a genuine love for all humankind.

## Chapter 13 – Letters

### LETTER #1

Rabbi Bulka was collecting toys for some needy children. He went to see my late Father. My Dad had a showroom at the time. Rabbi Bulka picked out some toys and then pulled out his wallet to pay for these. My Father refused payment but Rabbi Bulka fully intended to pay for what he selected.

---

1. Pirkay Avot 1:12, (Bulka, Ktav Publishing).

## LETTER #2

I have many stories of Rabbi Bulka's kindness but two stand out as particularly sweet.

When we first adopted our daughters they would go to shul Friday night with my husband. Each week they'd come home with a large plastic cup filled with candy, chocolate and cookies, announcing that Rabbi Bulka gave it to them. After a few weeks I spoke to Rabbi Bulka, suggesting maybe all that candy wasn't good for the girls. His response was "first I get them to like me, then I cut them off." Food, the gift of love.

In 2001 both Naomi Bulka and my sister were in hospital battling cancer. Rabbi Bulka would call me regularly, late at night, and we'd talk quietly, about many things. The details of our conversations are long forgotten but the comfort he brought me is with me still.

## OTTAWA'S FAITH LEADERS

We, the authors of this message to the people of the Nation's capital, come from different faith communities. But over the years we have worked together on many initiatives, including encouraging blood donation, signing up for organ and tissue donation, and taking part in Kindness Week, among others.

We firmly believe that in sharing the best of our faith traditions, we engender a spirit of cooperation in the community, and give tangible credence to the notion that religion in general is a unifier rather than a divider. We all know of the evil that has been perpetrated in the name of religion. We know less about the good that has been created and fostered by religion. We are united in our common belief that religions working together can achieve enormous good, and engender lasting cooperativeness.

We have once again joined together, in that embracing spirit, to work toward enhancing the life-saving efforts of all levels of government, all helping organizations, and all people of good will, in the humanitarian effort to save the lives of the multitude of refugees who are in desperate straits.

We have a great history in this regard. So many people and organizations put in a spectacular effort with Project 4000, a moment in Ottawa history that we all look back to with great pride. We are hopeful that we will be able to do the same with the present crisis that we all face together.

For those who may be too young to remember, Project 4000 came about in 1979, under the leadership and inspiration of then-Mayor Marion Dewar. After the collapse of South Vietnam in 1975, a half million Vietnamese fled their homeland, half of them by sea. Canada chose to accept thousands, and the late Marion Dewar felt that Ottawa, then a city of 400,000, could welcome and help settle 4,000 refugees. She had confidence in the people of our capital city, and the city more than justified that confidence. Quite likely, an older relative or friend of those who are reading this was involved. It was Ottawa at its glorious best.

We recognize that there are complicated issues. We are not here to criticize. We are here to jointly encourage. All of us have been uplifted by the spontaneous outburst of concern, and the overwhelming desire to help.

When members of all sectors of the community work together, the community itself benefits. A sense of community is forged, and the impact stays for a long time. Today, as the community contemplates its action plan, the model of Project 4000 jumps to the fore as the template for today. And the cooperative spirit of years ago has once again become a vibrant presence.

Ready means having open hearts to welcome and guide [refugees], open homes to house them, open wallets to support them, so that they can become good and appreciative Canadians. We do this for no other reason than it is the right, the upright, the proper and appropriate thing to do.

This is something that no matter where we come from on the faith grid, we can all believe in and embrace.

Archbishop Terrence Prendergast, Ottawa Diocese
Imam Samy Metwally, Ottawa Main Mosque
Rabbi Reuven P. Bulka, C.M., Rabbi Emeritus,
Congregation Machzikei Hadas

(Excerpted from an article published in The Ottawa Citizen, September 11, 2015, titled "We must all join together to help refugees"[1])

1. Excerpted from "We Must All Join Together to Help Refugees," *The Ottawa Citizen,* September 11, 2015.

## Chapter 14

# Faith and Building Bridges

> "The strangers who reside with you shall be to you as your citizens; you shall love each one as yourself, for you were strangers in the land of Egypt."
>
> – *(Leviticus 19:34, Sefaria)*

Rabbi Bulka was always known as a "bridge builder," connecting people who might otherwise not have been joined together. It didn't matter to Rabbi Bulka how observant someone was in their Judaism, as much as it didn't matter what religion a person practiced or if they practiced any religion at all.

"Ultimately," my grandfather expressed in a podcast with Mark Sutcliffe, "this isn't about who wins the religion race, but it's about getting them to focus on what's important in life and commit to making the world a better place. [This] underlines all religions. How can you make the totality [of humanity] better... [I] never in my life found that conflict solves problems... so much is accomplished by people cooperating with and getting along with each other. We all want the world to be a better place for everyone else, so let's just do it."

Thankfully, my grandfather had the opportunity to work with many religious leaders who felt the same way.

(Most Reverend) Terrence Prendergast, S.J., Emeritus Archbishop of Ottawa-Cornwall and Apostolic Administrator of Hearst-

Moosonee, shared his reflections and memories of Rabbi Bulka and the interfaith projects they worked on together[2]:

> "At his passing, Rabbi Reuven Bulka was hailed as 'Canada's Rabbi.' I liked to think of him as my Rabbi as well.
>
> He was, as well, a friend and a colleague in ministry.
>
> As a Jesuit priest and professor at Regis College at the Toronto School of Theology and in association with the University of Toronto, I was well acquainted with the Hebrew Bible, the New Testament and the world of intertestamental literature. That may have been why the Archbishop of Toronto named me to the Christian-Jewish Dialogue of Toronto on which I served happily for fourteen years (1981–95), two of them as co-chair.
>
> Christians and Jews dialogued, argued, wept and rejoiced together during those times. Christians and Jews, we have had painful relationships over the centuries, but thankfully channels of communication have been opened up in recent decades.
>
> Moving out of the world of academia, first as an auxiliary bishop in Toronto (1995–1998) and then as an archbishop in Halifax (1998–2007), changed the amount of time I had available for interfaith activities. I entrusted most of the responsibilities in these spheres to collaborators who had training in interfaith relations and who would keep me informed and ensure that I take part in significant occasions such as lectures at the Atlantic School of Theology or observances such as memorials of Kristallnacht and Holocaust Remembrance Week.
>
> When I came to Ottawa in 2007, my director of Interfaith Relations here invited me to a meeting of leaders of various faith communities; there I met Rabbi Bulka for the first time. As he had an effusive and engaging personality, it did not take long for us to strike up a conversation and agree that we might want to collaborate on addressing community issues.
>
> Having begun to read Rabbi Bulka's Saturday columns in the *Ottawa Citizen* under the heading "Ask the Religion Experts," I

2. Most Reverend Terrence Prendergast, personal communication

experienced a sense of fellowship with his thoughtful and practical approach to faith questions. When he reflected as a chaplain each Remembrance Day at the cenotaph, I had no difficulty in saying 'Amen' to his message and his prayer.

And, of course, Rabbi Bulka's horizons were always expanding as he reached out constantly to include other pastors and religious leaders, in particular an Imam. Thus it was that he and I and Imam Samy Metwally would reflect together on issues such as the proposal for legal measures to permit assisted suicide or euthanasia, which our religious traditions found abhorrent. We also wished to urge protection for medical personnel so they could refuse to participate in medical procedures that violated their conscience.

When acts of violence or hate-based gestures hurt members of other religious confessions, we made common cause in supporting the offended communities.

We also shared each other's joys. When the Canadian Jewish Experience exhibition was launched as part of Canada's sesquicentennial, I was pleased to attend. Later, by arranging for the exhibition to be shown for two weeks at the Ottawa archdiocesan centre, we permitted Catholics and others to have an opportunity to view it.

When the Archbishop of Riga, Latvia visited Ottawa and expressed an interest in learning about our interfaith activities in Ottawa, I was honoured to welcome Rabbi Bulka and other faith leaders to the Archbishop's Residence.

Rabbi Bulka's enthusiasm for the manifold acts of kindness that human beings can perform for each other led him to promote the establishment of 'Kindness Week,' working with school children to establish patterns of kindness early in life and extending it widely to other members of the civic community. To bring this home, he invited faith leaders and school children to join him at the international airport in welcoming visitors (or those returning home) to Ottawa with a warm greeting and the gift of a chocolate wrapped in gold-coloured foil.

Kindness Week activities take place in the third week of February. Initially, it was to begin on Wednesday. However, the first occasion would have fallen on Ash Wednesday; I said, 'Rabbi, that's like giving out candy on Yom Kippur.' So we moved it to Tuesday – Mardi Gras – a festive day for Catholics.

Our last project together fell a few weeks after the 2020 Kindness Week. It was an initiative to invite people of faith across Canada to pray for an end to the Covid-19 pandemic, for those researching a cure, for the front-line medical staff who were overwhelmed with patients in need of care, and for truckers and grocery store clerks and any others putting their lives on the line. We collaborated on its composition and I oversaw a French translation.

Through our joint efforts and invitations posted on social media, many thousands of Canadians joined in the prayer we had composed and which we recited jointly from the grounds of his synagogue: he in English and I in French.

I was very sad when I learned earlier this year of his cancer diagnosis and kept him in my prayers and thoughts until his passing. We are the same age (I am a few months older), and I sent him a message for his easy-to-remember birthday (he was born on D-Day). His reply, even at that difficult time in his final illness, was cordial and respectful. I shall treasure it.

May these recollections and those of many others ensure that the memory of this man of God remain a blessing to all who knew of him or had the pleasure of meeting him."

Bishop Shane Parker also reflected on his interactions with Rabbi Bulka. Bishop Parker first interacted with Rabbi Bulka through writing for the *Ottawa Citizen*, in the "Ask the Religions Expert" section of the newspaper. Bishop remarked that "even though we wrote from different faith traditions, we had the similar goal of serving the common good."

Any time a hate crime was committed, Bishop Parker and Rabbi Bulka tried to be visibly present together. Bishop Parker recalled that incidents of racism pushed their relationship into overdrive because it became evident that faith leaders needed to stand together.

In speaking to Bishop Shane, he told me that my grandfather was extremely focused on acceptance and hated the word "tolerance." According to Bishop Shane, "He was a person who spoke to people of all faiths and also of no faiths. He spoke of kindness and morality, and served those who were disenfranchised. He was highly respected. In fact, Bishop Shane told me that my grandfather often told off Christians for being too shy about Christmas. He would say, "I'll wish you a Merry Christmas and you can wish me a Happy Hanukkah."

"Especially between myself and your grandfather," Bishop Shane told me, "our differences were expressed very respectfully so you can accept it." What they had in common was their belief in a civil society and values of kindness and service and compassion.

Bishop Shane reminisced soberly about the horrible 9/11 attacks on the World Trade Center in New York City. He said that the prime minister of Canada ensured that leaders of all faiths were present on Parliament Hill. Bishop Shane and my grandfather were among those leaders, standing together with the leaders of government in a moment of silence. "We stand together in our tradition and accept the fact that we come from different places"[3].

Rabbi Bulka's "bridge building" expanded far into the world of advocacy. Rabbi Bulka was someone who advocated for a cause well before it was the "trendy" thing to do.

In Jewish tradition, in order to obtain a divorce, the husband must give his wife a certain document, called a "*get*," which will allow the divorce to proceed. There are unfortunately some men in the community who have abused this *get* and used it as a bargaining chip in divorces, effectively "chaining" their wives to dead marriages.

Long before this issue was brought to the forefront, Rabbi Bulka was passionate about making changes in Canadian law in order to make it more difficult for abusive men to get away with their "shenanigans" (as Rabbi Bulka would say). Rabbi Bulka testified before parliamentary hearings in Ottawa, alongside John Syrtash, in order to help pave the way for an easier Jewish divorce system in Canada. Accord-

3. Shane, Interview

ing to the *Canadian Jewish News*, "The amendments to the Divorce Act, which prevented recalcitrant Jewish (and Muslim) husbands from using a religious divorce as a bargaining chip in civil proceedings, passed unanimously in 1990".[4]

During the same time period, Rabbi Bulka also directed his advocacy work towards freeing Jews from the Soviet union.

Rabbi Bulka often organized rallies in front of the Soviet embassy in Canada. Many recall Rabbi Bulka shouting on a megaphone and rallying the crowd around the important cause.

After one rally that Rabbi Bulka had organized, an article came out in a local newspaper with a picture of Rabbi Bulka's youngest son, Binyomin. In the picture's caption, it explained that Binyomin was sitting and watching the rally. Following in the footsteps of Rabbi Bulka, where every word truly mattered, Binyomin wrote a letter to the newspaper to correct them: he wasn't simply watching the rally, he was participating.

While freedom for Soviet Jewry was a hot button issue in the latter part of the 20th century, many simply paid lip service to the cause. Rabbi Bulka took action.

Wendy Eisen, a dynamic Canadian leader involved in the cause of Soviet Jewry, wrote an enlightening book entitled *COUNT US IN – The Struggle to Free Soviet Jews: A Canadian Perspective.* Eisen generously shared her recollections on my grandfather's role in Soviet Jewry with me, and even sent me a copy of her book, of which I will share a few relevant excerpts.

Eisen (1997) remembers:

> In the early 1980s, Rabbi Bulka was Co-Chair of the Ottawa Committee for Soviet Jewry. In that position he was an outspoken advocate for the liberation of Soviet Jewry and he and I had a great deal of contact, since I was a "career Soviet Jewry activist" from 1974 when I lived in Montreal, as well as when I moved back to Toronto in 1981 until the gates parted in 1991.
>
> As an esteemed leader in Ottawa, Rabbi Bulka had the ear of

4. *Canadian Jewish News*, August 4, 2021.

many Members of Parliament who, through the Canadian Parliamentary Group for Soviet Jewry, chaired by MP David Kilgour, were helpful in speaking at demonstrations and encouraging Canadian officials to make representation on behalf of individual refuseniks to the Soviet authorities.

Rabbi Bulka was helpful in the Ottawa launch of my book: *COUNT US IN – The Struggle to Free Soviet Jews.* The event took place in the House of Commons on November 7, 1995, to which Members of Parliament, active in the Soviet Jewry campaign, and many Ottawa community members were invited[1].

Eisen explains:

> In the mid 1980s, during a period of time as emigration figures from the Soviet continued to decline, the Soviet Jewry campaign risked becoming a casualty of the "attrition of interest" syndrome.
>
> Rabbi Reuven Bulka warned that apathy played right into Soviet hands. "*The Russians are not comfortable when their anti-Semitism, their stifling of the fundamental rights of the Jews in Russia occupy world attention,*" Bulka wrote in *The Ottawa Jewish Bulletin and Review*. "*As matters get worse in Russia, instead of increasing the intensity of our protest efforts, we have moved away from involvement. That threatens to make us victims of Soviet strategy.*
>
> When the Christian Embassy produced a docudrama of the *Gates of Brass,* a film about the repression of Soviet Jewry, Rabbi Bulka commented on it:
>
> > "*Gates of Brass* is a superb portrayal that heightens the issue of Soviet Jewry for thousands of Canadians," wrote Rabbi Reuven Bulka, co-chairman of Ottawa's Soviet Jewry committee. "Through enactments of oppressive policies of the Soviet regime, remarkably frank statements of refuseniks and historical vignettes, a clear and concise picture of the condition of Soviet Jewry emerges."

---

1. Eisen, Wendy, *Count Us in: The Struggle to Free Soviet Jews: a Canadian Perspective*, (Burgher Books, 1995).

Reflecting on the miracle of progress with Soviet Jewry, in October 1989 during a march outside the Soviet Embassy, Rabbi Bulka commented:

> "It's difficult to imagine coming here and being grateful for progress. But this is truly a new era for Soviet Jews – to think of what has happened now is nothing short of a miracle."[2]

Following the rally, participants sang Israeli songs and held signs reading, "Let's keep the doors open." Bulka exchanged greetings with embassy guards and invited them to join the marchers for hot drinks.

* * *

Yet another example of Rabbi Bulka's ability to bridge gaps:

When Israel and Egypt first made peace in 1979, Rabbi Bulka invited the Egyptian ambassador to Canada to speak at his synagogue in order to bridge the gap between Jews and Arabs. Most people would not attempt this, as the mere notion of it asks for trouble.

It was a tense evening on the Friday night that the ambassador came to speak; the delicate history between Egypt and Israel and the differing opinions of shul members was palpable.

When Rabbi Bulka was around, there wasn't such a thing as an "awkward situation." Rabbi Bulka got up to introduce the Egyptian ambassador and said, "Me and you have a lot in common. They call me a-rab (a reference to the fact that some people called him Rab, short for Rabbi) and you a-rab." Everyone in the shul, the ambassador included, started to laugh and slowly watched the tensions melt away. In the end, it was an enjoyable and informative weekend for all who were present.

During the mourning period after Rabbi Bulka's passing, an impressive looking man joined the Zoom room that had been set up for the family, and everyone was shocked when they learned who this man was.

His name was Reverend Majed El Shafie. He had been sentenced

---

2. Ibid.

to death in Egypt for converting to Christianity and narrowly escaped through Israel, finally seeking political asylum in Canada. He explained that growing up in Egypt, one was indoctrinated on the evils of the Jewish people and Israel from a young age. El Shafie explained that in the school system, the media, and everywhere around them, antisemitic and anti-Zionist propaganda was shared in troves. When El Shafie attended the *shiva* (7-day mourning period) of Rabbi Bulka, he said, "Rabbi Bulka would call me his priest, and I would call him my Rabbi. I know you lost a father, husband, and friend. I lost a father figure and mentor and I feel it is my responsibility to tell you how great a man he was."

El Shafie explained that he and Rabbi Bulka fought side-by-side, he against antisemitism, and Rabbi Bulka against Christian persecution in the Middle East. Rabbi Bulka, according to El Shafie, single-handedly changed his viewpoint on the Jewish people and on Israel.

El Shafie poignantly ended his virtual visit by expressing, "I am consoled that he is in a better place than all of us with no agony, pain or fear – he is with his Lord, and I know he is in a better place than all of us and that it's never goodbye, it's see you soon. I will see my Rabbi again."

When Rabbi Bulka became ill, a Worldwide Prayer Rally was quickly organized by Rabbi Scher. While under difficult circumstances, the rally demonstrated Rabbi Bulka's ability to build bridges. The speakers included members of different political parties, including former Canadian Prime Minister Stephen Harper, former Ontario Premier Dalton McGuinty and then Mayor of Ottawa Jim Watson. It included Jewish, Christian and Muslim clergy and a diverse representation of the Jewish community. The 1000s of attendees represented an equally diverse cross-section of the global population. It is hard to imagine anyone else who could have brought together so many people with such different backgrounds, united for a single cause. While the circumstances of the rally were obviously extremely challenging, in many ways it encapsulated everything Rabbi Bulka strived for during his lifetime.

* * *

As explained earlier, Rabbi Bulka did not support a cause because it was popular but because he felt it was just. The oppressive treatment of certain minority groups in China was an issue about which my grandfather was extremely passionate. Rabbi Bulka wrote many articles criticizing the Chinese government and its treatment of certain members of society, one which I have included below that appeared in *The Ottawa Citizen* in July of 2019. In fact, he cared so deeply about this issue that he refused to purchase any item made in China, an obviously difficult feat in today's world.

What exactly was my grandfather's issue with China? Rabbi Bulka penned countless articles on the subject, but here is an excerpt from one that clearly expresses the problem:

> First, they denied. Then, they said they would stop it.
>
> Now, it turns out that they never did stop it. The ugly, murderous practice continues unchecked.
>
> I speak of the loud denial by Chinese authorities that they were "harvesting" organs from political prisoners, mainly the Falun Gong, to sell on the open market to people in need of organs.
>
> This is murder, brutal murder: taking organs from the bodies of live people because those organs are the freshest and best. Even though there was irrefutable evidence this was happening, the Chinese authorities denied it. This heinous practice was originally called out by Canadians David Matas and David Kilgour in their famous report of their painstaking research.
>
> Then, in 2014, in a horrible stain on the international community, the Chinese authorities announced they would soon be stopping this practice of taking organs from executed prisoners (i.e. taking organs and thereby executing prisoners). They announced stoppage of a practice they had previously denied. They said, for the entire world to hear: The murders of which we are accused, and which we deny ever happened, will soon stop!
>
> They thereby revealed that they are liars as well as murderers. No surprise that murderers are also liars. If life is cheap, the truth is even cheaper.

It is mind-boggling to think that the civilized "world" applauded, rather than calling out the Chinese government and demanding they stop the murders immediately rather than eventually. That remains a truly horrible stain.

The stain is even worse now, that based on a recent report, strangely not prominent in the Western press, we learn that the Chinese authorities are at it again, or more accurately, still at it. Can we be surprised that murderers have continued their ways, even though promising to stop?

Consider the painfully graphic statement of Sir Geoffrey Nice QC, Chair of the China Tribunal in London, tasked with investigating Chinese organ-harvesting practices, that appeared June 17 in *The Guardian*: "The conclusion shows that very many people have died indescribably hideous deaths for no reason, that more may suffer in similar ways and that all of us live on a planet where extreme wickedness may be found in the power of those, for the time being, running a country with one of the oldest civilizations known to modern man."

The facts are clear. Ninety-thousand transplants a year, coupled with a waiting time of just a few weeks and the assurance of a back-up organ should the original organ fail, is a combination that has no equal anywhere. That is the reality in China, and as Matas and Kilgour correctly pointed out, can only be explained as resulting from the murders of readily available "prisoners" – mostly members of the Falun Gong, but including Tibetans, Uighur Muslims and Christian sects.

Predictably, the Chinese Embassy in London responded by saying, "The Chinese government always follows the World Health Organization's guiding principles on human organ transplant, and has strengthened its management on organ transplant... providing that human organ donation must be done voluntarily and gratis..." The facts reveal the lie.

Alas, human rights abuses proliferate around the world. People are murdered daily. Often, there is little we can do. But with this situation, there are no excuses. We have some muscle, and we must use it. Governments must hold the Chinese government to account.

A number of countries ban travel to China for transplant surgery. Strangely, Canada and the United States are not among them. They should be.

No deal with a murderous regime that regularly kills its citizens to make money is worth the paper on which it is written. Any deal with China, on any matter, must include an insistence that this barbaric practice stop immediately, coupled with a mechanism whereby such stoppage is verifiable.

We, who rush to buy Chinese products, should ask ourselves if we are thereby supporting murder, even though that is surely not our intention. Maybe we can send a life-saving message by refusing to buy Made in China products if we can help it. Imagine saving lives merely through a change in buying habits. It sends a loud message, and is a profound manifestation of caring.

* * *

In Jewish history, Alexander the Great, the former king of Macedonia, was considered a great friend to the Jewish people, having met with Jewish leaders and who allowed the Jewish people to continue service in their holy temple. To show their gratitude to Alexander, the Jews began naming their sons "Alexander," and it has since been adopted as a Jewish name.

My husband and I were privileged to give birth to a baby within the first year of my grandfather's death, and we chose to name him Reuven Pinchas Alexander. Reuven Pinchas was my grandfather's full Hebrew name, and Alexander was an addition that my husband and I felt spoke to my grandfather's truest essence, a man who bridged faiths together and brought more unity and meaning into the world.

* * *

Frankl believed that faith could be a powerful force for good in the world, and that it can help to bring people together across different cultures and backgrounds. He believed that faith can be a powerful tool for promoting understanding, tolerance, and compassion among different people.

> It was characteristic of Frankl to accept individuals regardless of their religious beliefs or secular convictions. His deep commitment to the uniqueness and dignity of each individual was illustrated by his admiration for Freud and Adler even though he disagreed with their philosophical and psychological theories.[3]

This is exactly what Rabbi Bulka did. Like Frankl, he emphasized the importance of understanding and respect for different beliefs and traditions. He encouraged individuals to learn about and appreciate the beliefs of others, and to find shared values.

Remarkably, Rabbi Bulka's commitment to inclusivity extended to the creation of a prayer specifically dedicated to the welfare of Canada. This prayer was integrated into Jewish prayer services on the Sabbath, reflecting his unwavering belief in the importance emphasized in *Pirkay Avot* to "Pray for the welfare of the government,"[4] even when different beliefs, religions, and backgrounds are present. Below, you will find the text of his prayer, which beautifully encapsulates his ability to transcend personal boundaries and selflessly think of and pray for the well-being of others:

> May God, Who has blessed our patriarchs and matriarchs, bestow blessing upon the Governor-General, the Prime Minister, and the Government of Canada.
>
> Grant them ***wisdom*** and ***courage*** in these challenging times.
>
> Bless them with the ***wisdom*** to properly guide our beloved country.
>
> Imbue them with ***courage*** in their efforts to strengthen Canada.
>
> *And may we all together continue to experience Canada resolute in its togetherness and cooperative in its diversity.*
>
> **AMEN.**

Through his inclusive mindset and selfless actions, Rabbi Bulka demonstrated his profound commitment to embracing the larger community and fostering unity among diverse groups. His prayer serves as a testament to his compassionate and inclusive approach, inspiring

---

3. Frankl, Afterword, *Man's Search for Meaning*, 153.
4. Pirkay Avot 3:2, (Bulka, Ktav Publishing).

others to look beyond their own religious and cultural boundaries and actively contribute to the well-being of society as a whole.

## Chapter 14 – Letters

### LETTER #1

Andrea Freedman
Jewish Federation of Ottawa
July 2, 2021

Dear Ms. Freedman,

On behalf of the more than 25 member religious and spiritual communities of The Canadian Multifaith Federation (CMF), please accept our profound regret and sorrow on the passing of the eminent and beloved Rabbi Reuven Bulka. We respectfully request that you extend our sympathy to and through The Jewish Federation of Ottawa to the Jewish communities in Canada and beyond.

A loss of such magnitude tends to focus our hearts and minds on that which has been taken away. Yet we are determined to remember first Rabbi Bulka's many gifts both to the Jewish world and to his friends and neighbours of many faiths.

It is hardly an exaggeration to observe that Rabbi Bulka bestrode his world like a colossus. Rabbi, scholar, spiritual leader, publicist, diplomat, compassionate counsellor, good friend and neighbour: he was all these and more.

CMF's Ambassador-at-Large, the Rev. Prof. James Christie, has recalled Rabbi Bulka to us appreciatively and fondly. We are reminded of Rabbi Bulka's role as the Dean of the multifaith columnists who reflected weekly on religious questions in the Ottawa Citizen.

Rabbi Bulka was a key advisor to the United Church of Canada in the drafting of Mending the World. This ground-breaking study changed the nature not only of the relationship between The United Church of Canada and Judaism, but advanced Jewish-Christian dialogue worldwide.

Rabbi Bulka's warmth and friendship transcended religious differences. On one occasion, the Rabbi delayed his own Purim festivities to visit Dr. Christie's congregation in a demonstration of Christian-Jewish friendship.

We know well that such testimony could easily be multiplied a thousand-fold.

CMF joins you and the Jewish world in mourning this extraordinary Rabbi to the Global Village. Even more, we join you in giving thanks for his transcendent life and legacy.

Truly, God is good.
Yours Sincerely,

Pandit Roopnauth Sharma
President

### LETTER #2

My name is Imam Abdul Hai Patel, and I am a resident of Toronto, Canada, serving as Imam and community leader for 52 years.

I never thought that this moment will come this early that brought grief to me personally and to the Bulka family in particular and the Jewish committee in general.

I have known Rabbi Bulka for over 25 years. In 1996, I was introduced to him over a Kosher dinner, by the Vice President of Canadian Jewish Congress, the predecessor of CIJA, as a first step to formalize Muslim Jewish relations in Canada. He was the first Rabbi I met in my life and his personality, openness and humour paved the way for a long formal relationship with CJC.

Rabbi Bulka and I have shared several platforms for interfaith dialogues, meetings and human rights forums. His departure leaves a big void in the Rabbinical circles as well as in the community for promoting and enhancing pluralism, diversity and human rights. It is now up to us to uphold his legacy by recalling his enormous contribution to Canada and World Jewry.

I can't imagine how empty it will feel in Multifaith forums without him by my side. Our relationship was built with kindness and love, and evolved to share many platforms, gatherings and other activities together over the years. With his passing, he is leaving behind a legacy of kindness, compassion, and generosity.

Rabbi Bulka shared good humour and a big smile with everyone he met. Even though people often got upset at his practical jokes, he was an integral part of creating a solid foundation of friendship with many faith communities.

Anyone who met Rabbi Bulka quickly learned that there are always laughs to be shared. It was impossible to spend time with him without enjoying a gut-busting laugh at some point in the conversation.

I would like to thank the Bulka family for giving me this opportunity to express my grief and sadness at losing a pillar of support for my Interfaith activities. Please accept my deepest condolences to all those who are in grief at his departure from this world.

May his soul rest in peace.

Thank you.

## LETTER #3

Never in the history of my life have I met a more genuine, generous person, with a beautiful heart, more than you.

I was taught in the schools to consider the Jewish people to be my enemy. From a young age they taught me how to hate the Jewish people, but through my experiences in life, and belief in Christ as a Christian and through my friendship with you and many people in the Jewish community, that changed my heart and my attitude. One of those people was Anna-Lee Chiprout who is now my International Communications Director and Board Member of One Free World International. She was the person who introduced us and so began a very special friendship.

We did many events together but the most recent and meaningful was when you hosted it in your home. With the help of Anna-Lee, you and Stephen Victor invited special friends to a fundraiser. Thank God It was very successful and with that money we were able to rescue more girls who were kidnapped by ISIS, raped, beaten, then sold as sex slaves.

Your impact on my life personally and your fighting side by side with me against the persecution of the Christians and the rising of anti-semitism became one of the highlights in my life, and you became to me a close friend, a mentor, a father figure, but above all, my Rabbi.

Rabbi Bulka, I will not encourage you with empty words, but I will remind you of the God we worship and believe in. With all the medical reports and all the odds and numbers, sometimes we forget that there is a higher power, a God that loves us more than we love Him. God sees us more than we see Him or hear Him. A God that has miracles happen every day. Every breath we take is a miracle. Every new day is a miracle. Every hope is a miracle. A God that remembers and cares about every fish in every ocean, every bird on every tree and every ant under a piece of rock. And for that he will not forsake us.

I end this to you with a promise that I will see you again and with a promise that you will always be my Rabbi.

## LETTER #4

My wife Jenny and I were married in Toronto by a Reform Rabbi. She was not then Jewish and I had grown up in a completely secular Jewish home with practically no religious knowledge. A few years later, when she was pregnant, we thought it would be better for her to be converted and the child to be born Jewish. We did not know any Ottawa Rabbis. We asked around, and phoned Rabbi Bulka, who was then recently arrived in Ottawa. He came to our home, and agreed to make arrangements for Jenny to be converted. I said that I felt bad, leaving such an important matter to the last minute. Rabbi Bulka said at once, "That's nothing unusual. You wake up when the alarm clock rings." That was, as I learned over the years, a typical Rabbi Bulka comeback. After the conversion he invited us to his home, where we were married again under a Chupa that he set up in his front hall. That was in 1973. Our family experienced Rabbi Bulka's warmth and welcome in many ways in the years since.

## LETTER #5

While I have had the pleasure of many wonderful interactions with the Rabbi over the last few years that he chaired the campaign, my fondest memory is from when I had just moved to Ottawa 25 years ago and was having my Bar Mitzvah. Ever gracious, Rabbi B invited me to come participate in morning minyan at CMH, which for the son of the new Reform Rabbi in town was incredibly meaningful to both me and my father.

## *Chapter 15*
# Simple, Yet Extraordinary

"Simplicity is the ultimate sophistication."

– *Leonardo da Vinci*

To many, when they think of kindness and going above and beyond, they immediately start to think of lofty ways that one can be kind: joining charity organizations, chairing fundraisers, visiting the sick. While Rabbi Bulka was involved in the "bigger things," it is the endless amount of "smaller things" that truly gave Rabbi Bulka a legacy of kindness.

Over the seven-day mourning period following Rabbi Bulka's death, many stories were shared with our family that we had never heard before.

A man, we'll call him Joe, was having a difficult week and was struggling to keep himself from reaching a state of panic and uncontrollable anxiety. He did everything he could to keep distance from the people around him. He went to shul, smiled as he usually did, and made his way home.

Then came *Leil Shabbat* (Friday evening). Things that regularly wouldn't have bothered Joe reached heightened levels of sensitivity.

Joe and the rest of the congregation went to shake Rabbi Bulka's hand after prayer services. Innocently, my grandfather attempted to *kibbitz* (joke around) with Joe like usual, but Joe was unable to receive his kind humor the way it was intended. "I didn't mean to," Joe recalled, "but I ended up making very little eye contact and rushed home."

After a quiet *Shalom Aleichem* and *Kiddush,* Joe heard a firm knock on his door. Sure enough, it was Rabbi Bulka.

"Rabbi Bulka! What are you doing here?" Joe inquired, incredulous and slightly embarrassed. "It's late. Should you not be bringing in Shabbos already?"

He answered: "Reb Joe, how on earth could I welcome Shabbos knowing that Shabbos has not yet settled in your home?"

With that, Rabbi Bulka wished Joe a Good Shabbos. Joe gave him a hug, admittedly holding him a little tighter than usual.

Afterwards, Rabbi Bulka left, refusing to let Joe walk him out.

Rabbi Bulka was gone, but Shabbos was in.

* * *

This kind of story was not a one-time occurrence. The current Rebbetzin of Machzikei Hadas, Shifra Scher, recalled a similar experience happening to her. When she first arrived in Ottawa, she was having difficulty obtaining a work permit and was noticeably despondent about it. Rabbi Bulka, with his high level of emotional intelligence, picked up on this and arrived at her doorstep on Friday night following prayer services to make sure she was alright.

These are stories I had never heard before until the mourning period for Rabbi Bulka. I can only imagine how many more there must be.

Rabbi Bulka did not shy away from manual labor, and would do anything it took to make people feel more comfortable. He may have been head and shoulders above others in stature, but no task was too menial for him.

One shul member recalled a story that took place after her late mother passed away from cancer.

Her mother spent the last few weeks of her life receiving palliative care at home, and was loaned a hospital bed. When the health services came to retrieve the hospital bed following her mother's death, they did not bring her regular bed back into her bedroom.

Rabbi Bulka was there to assist with the funeral and later joined the family at the *shiva* (mourner's) home. The family was sitting in the living room and receiving guests with a huge bed obstructing the room.

Rabbi Bulka noticed this awkward situation and jumped up. He exclaimed: "We have got to move this bed back to its proper place." Like Superman and with a little bit of help from others, Rabbi Bulka *schlepped* (dragged) the bed back into its original place in the bedroom. The living room was immediately freed up for the many visitors that were filing through the front door.

Rabbi Bulka was always the one to notice a situation, point it out, and solve it. No task was too lowly or degrading. In fact, Rabbi Bulka delighted in being able to help in such ways.

As the family pointed out, "We are eternally grateful to Rabbi Bulka, who not only moves people spiritually but also moves furniture."

* * *

For many years, Rabbi Bulka had the opportunity, joined by his wife, Leah, to be the scholar-in-residence at The Fairmont Scottsdale Princess Passover Program in Scottsdale, Arizona. The couple who ran the Passover program for the previous ten years were nervous to meet the new Rabbi and his wife, especially since the Passover kitchen had to provide three daily meals and had a difficult time keeping up with special requests.

Rabbi Bulka had his own personal custom in which he did not eat any meat or chicken during the week, but made sure to eat something meat-related at each holiday meal. The owners of the Passover program weren't sure how they were going to accommodate this, but Rabbi Bulka made it easy. He didn't need a full meat meal, but instead was sent a refrigerator, a salami, and a paper plate, allowing him to keep his tradition without imposing on the kitchen staff.

This story exemplifies Rabbi Bulka – a man who was extremely principled but never imposed on others.

The Passover program owners reminisced about the way Rabbi Bulka would help them or any guest with help or advice. When the pandemic hit in 2020 and closed down all Passover programs, the owners recalled how Rabbi Bulka was worried about them and started writing to them each week before the Sabbath to make sure they were doing alright.

* * *

A family friend shared an experience that reminded me just how impactful an act of kindness can be. What's more, he made it clear that I hardly knew the magnitude of my grandfather's impact.

It was a Shabbat at a shul in Toronto, and my grandfather was the scholar-in-residence. Bucky Prizant, a native of Ottawa and close family friend, noticed someone he knew having a long conversation with Rabbi Bulka.

Following the conversation, Bucky asked how he knew Rabbi Bulka.

"I didn't," the man replied. "This is actually my first time meeting him in person. A few years ago, my marriage was in a very bad place. Someone had recommended we call Rabbi Bulka, and he literally saved our marriage. Ever since, Rabbi Bulka has called us every week to check in on how we are doing. So I had to take this opportunity to finally meet him in person and thank him."

In its very essence, logotherapy serves as a powerful tool to cultivate awareness of one's responsibility. While logotherapy itself may not explicitly outline the responsibility of initiating greetings to all people, Rabbi Bulka personally felt a strong sense of duty in doing so, drawing inspiration from the teachings of *Pirkay Avot.* As highlighted in *Pirkay Avot,* the directive to "be the initiator of greetings to all people"[5] resonated deeply with Rabbi Bulka, and he embraced it with utmost seriousness, as evidenced by the stories shared above.

In this way, Rabbi Bulka's personal interpretation and application of the teachings of *Pirkay Avot* align with the principles of logotherapy, as it highlights his conscious awareness of his role and responsibility in cultivating meaningful connections with others. By internalizing the wisdom of *Pirkay Avot,* Rabbi Bulka exemplified a deep sense of duty, demonstrating the profound impact that embracing such responsibilities can have on our lives and the lives of those around us.

---

5. Pirkay Avot 4:15, (Bulka, Ktav Publishing).

# Chapter 15 – Letters

## LETTER #1

There are many leadership lessons I learned from you that I try to mimic:

- Nothing is below you – I have seen you get chairs for people at events, serve food, clean up, etc…
- You are always in a good mood, smiling, warm, approachable, and embracing
- You inject humour as appropriate (puns, gematria, and combining the first letters of people's names usually!)
- Treat everyone the same regardless if they are "important" or not; and be accepting of every person
- When one-on-one, listen and do not be prescriptive unless absolutely necessary
- Think differently and big – I always liked your thinking around the Jewish University in Ottawa; and in our current shul campaign you always asked the most intriguing questions that made us all rethink
- Write things down to move a group of people forward – when I was working on merging the two frum schools, you told me to do this early on so both sides could see something concrete. It worked, and I continue to do that at work and in community projects
- No job, task, or mitzvah is too small – the most recent thing you did for me was tie my new tzizis to my Shabbos tallis; and I remember you fixing my tefillin before my Bar Mitzvah (my Shel Yad still has a piece of cardboard from your house!)
- Donate blood and organs – I do this because of you. I have donated blood over 70 times and have offered my organs to others twice before….
- Be careful with words and saying nothing is often best – I imagine this is why you chose the pasuk of "Kol demama daka" on the brass panels next to the Ahron

## LETTER #2

Dear Rabbi Bulka,

Throughout my life you have magically appeared at the hospital bedside of my parents and siblings to brighten one's day. You are a goodwill ninja. This world needs so many more of you.

## LETTER #3

I have been to many funerals at which Rabbi Bulka officiated. He always makes sure that the grave is fully covered over before the people leave. I have been to funerals elsewhere, where the coffin is lowered into the grave and a few shovelfuls of earth are thrown on it and then the people leave it to the cemetery workers to finish the job. Rabbi Bulka's meticulousness in this is an example of his kindness. It is kind to the deceased. It is kind to the family. And it is kind to the friends and all those attending, who are given an opportunity to perform a mitzvah.

*Chapter 16*

# Menachem Begin, the Queen of England, and Uncle Moishy

"One person can make a difference, and every person should try."

– *John F. Kennedy*

We all love a good story. When it comes to Rabbi Bulka, there are a few stories that I'd be remiss if I did not include in this volume. One such story is Rabbi Bulka's rendezvous with Prime Minister Menachem Begin.

Rabbi Bulka had met Menachem Begin before he became Prime Minister, and found him to be an authentic and serious individual.

When Begin came to Ottawa, Rabbi Bulka was responsible to ensure that the food for his visit was kosher. Rabbi Bulka was with Begin at a community reception dinner. As they were speaking, Menachem Begin was eating a shish kabob on a long stick and accidentally stuck the stick into his mouth from the wrong end. He was about to choke when Rabbi Bulka yanked the shish kabob out. Rabbi Bulka says he has no evidence that this story occurred, but that it was a highlight for him. Menachem Begin had not yet become Prime Minister of Israel, so perhaps we owe some of that to Rabbi Bulka?

Rabbi Bulka had the opportunity to meet with many world leaders, notably, the Queen of England, Queen Elizabeth II. The Queen was arriving in Toronto and Rabbi Bulka was invited to a special dinner in her honor. Prior to the dinner, they had received instructions on how to give courtesy to the Queen. Rabbi Bulka's wife, Leah Bulka, wore a formal gown, and the Bulkas received two of the four kosher meals served at the event.

There was a blackout in Ontario at the time, and Rabbi Bulka and his wife were staying on the tenth floor of their hotel. They quickly walked down ten flights to be in attendance for the dinner, but because the blackout caused delays, they each had only a few seconds to greet the Queen.

When Rabbi Bulka's turn came, he asked the Queen if he could make the blessing on royalty. She responded in the affirmative, and Rabbi Bulka recited the blessing in both Hebrew and English. She was very grateful and then moved on to meet the rest of the guests. After the event, people wondered what Rabbi Bulka had discussed with the Queen, considering each person only spent a few seconds courtesying.

Clearly, Rabbi Bulka had an impact regardless of who it was.

In fact, to quote my own father about Rabbi Bulka: "You wouldn't know who my father was talking to based on the way he would talk to people. It could've been the Prime Minister, the Queen, a gas attendant, a barista- it was all the same to him, they were all people and all worthy of equal kindness." He embodied the essence of *Pirkay Avot's* call to action: "Greet all people with a cheerful countenance,"[1] regardless of stature.

* * *

Though not world-renowned, "Uncle Moishy" has been a classic among Jewish children everywhere since 1975. Leave it to Rabbi Bulka to have an impact on children's music.

One of "Uncle Moishy"'s more famous songs, called "Big Gedaliah Goomber," a song about not conducting work on the Sabbath, stirred my grandfather. The lyrics read[2]:

---

1. Pirkay Avot 1:15, (Bulka, Ktav Publishing).
2. Uncle Moishy and the Mitzvah Men, "Big Gedaliah Goomber," Volume 1, 2005.

I once helped raise a building
And on the hundredth floor
I was carrying a load of bricks
An easy ton or more...
And here, it's late on Friday
I knew I'd have to stop
So I yelled, "Watch out below!"
And let the whole thing drop.
Ohhhhh....

CHORUS:
Ain't gonna work on Saturday
Ain't gonna work on Saturday
Double, double, triple pay
Won't make me work on Saturday
Ain't gonna work on Saturday...
It's Shabbos Kodesh.

Rabbi Bulka was disturbed by these words, as he did not want young Jewish children to think that it was proper to drop a load of bricks and potentially hurt people under any circumstances. In true Rabbi Bulka fashion, he wrote a letter voicing his concerns.

I remember my father telling me this story when I was younger, and the story always left me wondering what ever happened to that letter.

Well, after my grandfather's passing, Zale Newman, the creator of Uncle Moishy, sent us this letter:

> B"H, I was blessed to have a relationship with Rabbi Bulka going back 45 years or more to my days with NCSY Eastern Canada in 1974 and beyond.
>
> In fact, I met my wife going to an NCSY Shabbaton in the spring of 1978 at Machzikei Hadas. We were married in Montreal later that year. We were very young and were two students. For our wedding, we received a bunch of cheques as wedding gifts. After the wedding and three sheva brachos, we went to Toronto where we were going to live and go to school. We still live here today almost 43 years later.

After we got home to our very first apartment, I asked my wife "What do you think we should do with all of this money"? (it wasn't really very much but to two students it sure seemed like a lot at the time). She replied, "Why don't we give a little tzedaka"? Well, I had played a lot of music and had written many songs and I was usually triggered by particular words. So I said, "Wait a minute," went into the next room and wrote a children's song called "Give a Little Tzedaka." Later that night I asked my wife what Jewish children's songs she knew from being a nursery school teacher and a camp counselor; and I knew some from my days in youth work. And I had written some, too.

So there were enough songs for an album. I called the music production team of Suki and Ding with whom I was friends and who had arranged the music for our wedding, and I gave them the idea of Uncle Moishy and the Mitzvah Men, and that is how a 40-year phenomenon, with 25 albums, 30 videos and many other products and world tours, began.

On the first album there was a song written by a Toronto songwriter called "Big Gedalia Goomber." It had been recorded on an obscure record album in 1965. We bought the rights to record it and used it on the first UM & MM album with follow up songs on two additional albums, too. The first UM & MM album was a huge hit, selling more than 50,000 copies, the 2nd most of any Jewish album in North American history.

One day we received a letter from Ottawa. It was from Rabbi Bulka *a"h*. He congratulated us on the album but then took the time to point out that we had to be meticulous in what we said as we could have a profound impact on how a young Jewish child thinks. In the song "Big Gedaliah Goomber" there is a verse where "BGG" was building a building and he was lifting a ton or more of bricks. But as it got close to Shabbos, he "let the whole thing drop" and ran home for Shabbos.

Rabbi Bulka pointed out that this was teaching a child to be irresponsible with someone else's items. Furthermore by dropping the bricks, one could hurt someone else and would certainly cause a huge mess.

We took Rabbi Bulka's teaching to heart. From that point on, through more than 250 song recordings, we were very meticulous with every word that we sang or spoke to try and measure how a child might hear and learn from what he or she had heard.

In all the years, almost no one else took the time to point out things in UM & MM that should have been corrected or said differently. Only Rabbi Bulka listened and then took the time out to correct what we had done. Thank you Rabbi Bulka!!! (I wonder how many millions of teachings he shared over the many years as a Rabbi/teacher/scholar/friend/leader....)

Simchas and sweet memories forever.

Zale Newman
Toronto

Clearly, Rabbi Bulka's influence knew no bounds.

*Chapter 17*

# Conclusion: Logotherapy in Action

"Suffering ceases to be suffering at the moment it finds a meaning."
– *Viktor Frankl*

The last six months of my grandfather's life were bittersweet. I got to spend more time with my grandfather than ever before, yet all the while acutely aware of the limited time we had left to spend together. Throughout his illness, Rabbi Bulka's trademark sense of humor remained intact. Rabbi Bulka joked with his doctors and brought them signed copies of his latest book. When he was quite sick and a nurse came and asked if she could take his blood pressure, he replied, "Sure, as long as you give it back."

It amazed me to watch Rabbi Bulka live his life to its fullest, even in the face of death. As Viktor Frankl wrote: "Everything can be taken from a man but one thing; the last of the human freedoms – to choose one's attitude in any given set of circumstances, to choose one's own way".[1]

Despite a grim prognosis, my grandfather did not become depressed. He told me that throughout his life at the pulpit, he had met with young mothers, children, and others who were diagnosed with fatal illnesses. Having encountered death on a near constant basis in

1. Frankl, *Man's Search for Meaning*, 61.

the Rabbinate, he felt blessed to have had a full life, or, as I should say, a meaningful life.

I've never met someone who practiced what he preached in the way that Rabbi Bulka did. He practiced logotherapy with his constituents, but he truly lived it, likely even before he knew it was a discipline.

I spent as many days as I could visiting and speaking with my grandfather at the end of his life. It was a privilege for me to mail letters for him, pick up *sefarim* (Jewish books) and do things for him that he no longer could.

I remember the last Friday of his life. I almost didn't go over, but my mother-in-law had shown me an article my grandfather had written that had come out that day in a popular Jewish magazine. I thought my grandfather might appreciate seeing it. I brought it over and before I left, my grandfather was able to muster the strength to say one last "Good Shabbos."

It felt like an ominous greeting, and after the Sabbath, we were notified that the time had likely come to say goodbye. I remember saying to him while squeezing his hand: "You have always been my hero." If there is anyone in the world with whom I share interests, it is him. I teach psychology, Judaic studies, and love to write about how they connect. There are so many times that I wish I could call my grandfather and seek his advice, his opinion, his humor.

After conducting so many interviews, I was envious of the fact that so many people were fortunate enough to have a relationship with my grandfather as adults, helping them navigate their adult lives. I am privileged to have had Rabbi Bulka in my life for 26 years, but it feels like I lost him right when I needed him most.

This book was how I found meaning in a pretty horrible situation. Once it became known that I was "writing a book," I was invited to record interviews, reached out to by many in the Ottawa community, and called upon to listen to different stories about his life. It gave me meaning while he was sick, it gave me meaning through the mourning period, and it continues to give me a strong connection to my grandfather and his life.

I lamented to my family that it would have been a lot easier if my grandfather would have kept a log or diary of his life somewhere on his computer, because only he could actually write about all his life's endeavors and accomplishments. Except that he wouldn't. He could never have known the impact of some of his kindness, and his humility prevented him from ever publicizing his accolades.

I am positive that the stories about Rabbi Bulka's kindness are endless, and that his vast impact is even further reaching than anyone can imagine.

It felt fitting to me to write about his life in the context of meaning, because that is how he lived, up until the very end.

As *Pirkay Avot* beautifully states, "One in whom the spirit of humankind takes delight, the spirit of the Omnipresent takes delight,"[2] encapsulating Rabbi Bulka's unwavering commitment to bringing joy and fulfillment to others, thereby finding favor not only with his fellow human beings but also with the Divine. His legacy of compassion and selflessness continues to inspire and resonate with all those fortunate enough to have encountered his remarkable presence. His profound influence serves as a reminder of the power of kindness and the enduring impact one person can have on the world.

As I wrote in the introduction, there is no way that one book could do his life justice. As Frankl so beautifully puts it:

> "We cannot, after all, judge a biography by its length, by the number of pages in it; we must judge by the richness of the contents... Sometimes the 'unfinisheds' are among the most beautiful symphonies".[3]

But one thing is clear.

I have taken the liberty of replacing the word "man," "he," and "his" with "Rabbi Bulka" in a quote written by Viktor Frankl:

> "Rabbi Bulka is unique in terms of both existence and essence. Rabbi Bulka is unique in that, in the final analysis, Rabbi Bulka

2. Pirkay Avot 3:10, (Bulka, Ktav Publishing).
3. Frankl, *Doctor and the Soul*, 66.

cannot be replaced. And Rabbi Bulka's life is unique in that no one can repeat it".[4]

4. Frankl, Viktor, *Feeling of Meaninglessness: A Challenge to Psychotherapy and Philosophy*, (Milwaukee, Wisconsin: Marquette University Press, 2010), 178.

# Acknowledgements

First and foremost, I must express my appreciation to God for endowing me with the necessary resources, fortitude, and creativity to complete this book. My grandfather, who lived a remarkable life, would have been the only person who could have authored this book with complete accuracy. I will always be grateful to God for the privilege of having been able to spend time with my grandfather, especially at the end of his life, and gather firsthand accounts of his experiences.

I could not have completed this book without the support and love of my husband, Daniel. His encouragement and belief in me have been one of the driving forces behind my success. His sacrifices and understanding have allowed me the time and energy to spend countless hours on the interview process and on writing. I am grateful for his love and patience, and for allowing me to be sappy in this paragraph.

Thank you to my wonderful children, Adi and Xander, who probably have no idea that I have been working on this, but are part of my journey, nonetheless. It gave me great joy to see Adi interact with my grandfather before he passed away, and I will always be grateful that I was able to name my second son after my grandfather within a year of his passing.

I am incredibly grateful to my parents for their love and support throughout my life, and especially during the writing of this book. My father's guidance and wisdom have been invaluable in allowing me to tell the story of his father in a way that is both accurate and respectful. His willingness to share his personal memories and experiences has added depth and richness to this book. He has been the sounding board throughout the entire editing process, and his unwavering commitment to see this project to its fruition is truly why you are holding this book in your hands. I am, of course, extremely grateful to my mother for her constant encouragement and for her unwavering belief in my abilities. Her love and support have been a constant source of inspiration throughout this book and beyond. There truly are not enough words to describe my appreciation for all that she has and continues to do for me and my family.

I am also incredibly grateful to my in-laws who have been a huge point of support since I joined the family, and who care about me like their own daughter. My mother-in-law is always happy and willing to engage in conversation about any topic, and she has been a great sounding board for concepts and ideas that I thought about including in this book. Of course, she is also always excited about the opportunity to watch my children, which has been instrumental in my being able to write this book. My father-in-law, too, is always a phone call away and doesn't mind (or at least pretends he doesn't mind) when I call him at any time of day or night with a medical question of some sort. He has helped keep my family physically healthy over the years, allowing me to focus on other things in my life (like writing this) and is always a great sounding board for discussing ideas.

I express my deepest gratitude to my grandparents: Grandma, Grandpa, and Bubbie Leah. I thank them for their unwavering support and encouragement throughout my life. They are always my biggest fans, there to chat with me and show genuine interest in everything I do. Their love and guidance mean the world to me and I thank them for being such wonderful grandparents.

I am deeply grateful to my siblings and siblings-in-law for their love and support, always. Their encouragement, understanding, and willingness to help in any way is greatly appreciated.

To my sister, Talia. Despite her crazy work schedule, she took the time to read through the manuscript and share her thoughts and edits, for which I am extremely grateful.

To my brother, Avi. My brother managed to get me access to any resource I was looking for before I could even finish asking. He helped me track down sources, people, and ideas, and offered guidance in the writing process as well.

And to my sisters and brothers in law who have always been and continue to be a huge point of support:

My sisters-in-law: Yehudis, Mikayla, and Rachel
My brothers-in-law: Avraham and Noam

I am blessed to have such supportive and loving siblings who have always been there for me. Thank you for being my support system, my confidants, and my family.

I am deeply grateful to my aunts and uncles: Aunt Yocheved and Uncle Moshe, Aunt Rena and Uncle Yehuda, Uncle Eliezer and Aunt Haviva, and Uncle Binyomin and Aunt Shira for their invaluable contributions to this book. Their personal memories, stories, and insights about their father have added meaning and depth to this book that would not have otherwise been possible. Their willingness to share their experiences and to open their hearts has been invaluable.

I offer further thanks to my uncle, Eliezer, for his invaluable editing skills in refining the book. His keen eye and thoughtful feedback have truly elevated the quality of the manuscript. As I mentioned in the text of the book, Eliezer did not hold back on comments, but shared them in the most helpful way possible. I am truly grateful for his input.

I extend my heartfelt gratitude to all the individuals who shared their stories and experiences with me during the research and interview process for this book:

Dr. Harry Prizant, Rabbi Idan Scher and Rebbetzin Shifra Scher, Dr. Aviva Freedman, David Freeman (aka Moose), Andrea Freedman, Bonnie Boretsky and Andrew Fainer, Dan Greenberg, Rabbi Chaim Boyarsky, Jeff Turner, Label Silver *a"h*, Ron Prehogan, Rabbi Moshe Drelich, Bishop Shane Parker, and Ronny Gavsie.

Their contributions and willingness to be open and candid about their experiences have been instrumental in bringing this book to life.

Thank those who went above and beyond in their willingness to participate in the research process:

> I extend my sincerest gratitude to Bram Bregman, who was always just an email away. Bram's unwavering willingness to help and his ability to find answers to any question, big or small, made him an invaluable point of contact throughout the writing process. His constant availability and adeptness at providing assistance truly put me at ease and allowed me to focus on writing. Bram's help was instrumental in making this book a reality, and I am deeply appreciative of his contributions. I wish you and your family all the best on your move to Israel.
>
> I offer further gratitude to Dr. Peggy Kleinplatz for illuminating the core principles of logotherapy and for her invaluable guidance in integrating them into this book. Prior to our conversations, the notion of incorporating logotherapy into a biographical account of my grandfather seemed like a far-fetched dream. However, Dr. Kleinplatz's expertise and insights on the subject opened my eyes to new perspectives; and I am grateful for the time she spent educating me and sharing her inspiring anecdotes about my grandfather. Further, Dr. Kleinplatz graciously edited the entire manuscript, employing her discerning eye and drawing from her own personal connection with my grandfather. Her contributions have been instrumental in shaping this book, and I am deeply indebted to her for her expertise and generosity.

Their time, effort, and willingness to share their knowledge and experience are greatly appreciated.

Thank you to Peter Waiser for generously sharing and allowing us permission to use many of his photographs for the book, including the cover photo. Thank you as well to Alex Sarna and Irving Osterer for sharing their photos as well, and allowing us to use them to enhance this volume.

Thank you to Abigail Lampert for her keen eye in designing the beautiful cover of this book. It has been a privilege getting to work with a former student on a professional level. Abigail's patience, efforts, and quality of work are unmatched in the design field. She worked with us until everyone was obsessed with the design, and truly wowed us.

I am deeply indebted to my editor and friend (and former teacher while we're at it) Shira Greenberger for her invaluable contributions to this book. Her expertise, guidance and unwavering support were instrumental in bringing this book to fruition. Without her, you would not be holding this in your hands. Her ability to identify the potential in my writing and her steadfast encouragement throughout the process were vital in keeping me motivated to see the project through to completion. I am grateful for her meticulous attention to detail, her dedication to elevating my manuscript, and her boundless patience. Her hard work and keen editorial eye were essential in taking this book to the next level. I cannot express enough gratitude for her invaluable help and support.

Thank you to Moshe Heller and Miriam Dichter from Ktav for all their help in making this book a reality. Given all the projects they have done with my grandfather over the years, Ktav is the perfect home for this book. I am indebted to them for their eagerness to take on this project and for allowing Rabbi Bulka's extraordinarily life to inspire as many people as possible.

I express my deep appreciation to The Viktor E. Frankl Institute of America for their educational courses on logotherapy. I am also profoundly grateful to Dr. Franz Vesley, Viktor Frankl's son-in-law, for granting me permission to use Viktor Frankl's writings. Additionally, I extend my heartfelt thanks to Alex Vesley, Viktor Frankl's grandson, for taking the time to engage in personal conversation with me and for generously providing invaluable comments on my utilization of logotherapy in the book, as well as insightful input on essential concepts within logotherapy. I am truly grateful for his overall feedback on the book and have appreciated the ability to gain a deeper understanding of the special bond between our grandfathers.

Thank you to Rabbi Shimon Fogel and Beatriz Roth whose invaluable support and dedication have been instrumental to enhancing this publication. Thank you as well to Bradley Dock whose keen editorial eye during the manuscript's final stages have contributed greatly to the overall quality of the book.

Thank you to all my family members and friends for their support and encouragement throughout the entire process. Thank you to all the individuals whom I have met over the last few years that provided invaluable insight into my grandfather's life. Thank you to those who took the time to write emails and letters, sharing their thoughts and stories, which have provided the most real insight into the lasting impact my grandfather had on all those whose lives he touched.

# About the Author

Rikki (Bulka) Ash is a passionate high school educator, teaching psychology, history, Tanakh (Bible), and prayer. She is also a Kallah teacher, dedicated to helping women transition into their new roles as wives and mothers. Inspired by her writing, Rikki founded "Rikki Ash Con**soul**ting," a coaching and consulting firm that empowers women to find meaning in their lives through logotherapeutic ideas. Alongside her grandfather, Rabbi Bulka, she co-authored "*Honeycombs: The Amidah Through the Lens of Rav Yonasan Eybishitz and Rav Yosef Hayyim of Baghdad*," delving into the topic of the amidah (silent daily prayer). Rikki considers her grandfather, Rabbi Bulka, her hero, and aspires to continue his legacy of integrating and teaching Judaism with psychology. Feel free to reach out at rikki@rikkiash.com or visit rikkiashconsoulting.com.

# Bibliography

Bulka, Reuven P. "Ask the Religions Expert," *Ottawa Citizen*, February 26, 2014.

Bulka, Reuven P. "Ask the Religions Expert," *Ottawa Citizen*, March 23, 2014.

Bulka, Reuven P. *Old Ideas for New Times*. Ottawa, J. Bulka Verlag Publishing House, 2013.

Bulka, Reuven P. "Op-ed," *Ottawa Citizen*, January 13, 2021.

Bulka, Reuven P. *Pirkay Avos on Marriage: Timely Ideas from a Timeless Source*. Brooklyn, NY: Ktav Publishing House, 2020.

Bulka, Reuven P. "We Must All Join Together to Help Refugees," *Ottawa Citizen*, September 11, 2015.

Bulka, Reuven P. *Work, Love, Suffering & Death: A Jewish/Psychological Perspective Through Logotherapy*. Ottawa: J. Aronson, 1997.

Bulka, Reuven P. *Turning Grief Into Gratitude*. Ottawa: Paper Spider, 2007.

Congregation Machzikei Hadas, accessed July 10, 2023, https://www.cmhottawa.com.

Eisen, Wendy. *Count Us in: The Struggle to Free Soviet Jews: A Canadian Perspective*. Burgher Books, 1995.

Frankl, Viktor E. *The Doctor and The Soul: From Psychotherapy to Logotherapy*. Second Vintage Books ed., New York, NY: Random House, Inc., 1986.

Frankl, Viktor E. *Man's Search for Meaning*. Boston, Massachusetts: Beacon Press, 2006.

Frankl, Viktor E., Man's Search for Ultimate Meaning. (New York: Perseus Publishing, 2000), 91. Kindle.

Governor General of Canada website, accessed on July 10, 2023, https://www.gg.ca/en_In Memory of Rabbi Bulka," Ottawa Regional Cancer Foundation, accessed July, 10 2023, https://www.ottawacancer.ca/in-memory-of-Rabbi-bulka/.

Noetic Films, "Reflection on Frankl," YouTube video, 09:17, posted May 13, 1920, https://youtu.be/uKpabqvcV-8.

## *Appendix A*

# Honors and Awards

Who is honored? One who honors mankind."

– *Pirkay Avot 4:1*

Rabbi Bulka was reluctant to accept honors and awards, and only did so with good reason.

When the Rabbi Bulka Kindness Park in Alta Vista was set to be dedicated in his honor, Rabbi Bulka was hesitant. First, he insisted that the word "kindness" be included in the naming. Rabbi Bulka was not interested in promoting himself but in promoting the principle of kindness. Rabbi Bulka also thought that having a park named for a Rabbi would keep the Jewish sentiment alive in Alta Vista, the Jewish community where he resided in Ottawa. Here is an excerpt from the Ottawa Jewish E-Bulletin that describes the circumstances behind this award[1]:

> "'For over 50 years, Rabbi Dr. Reuven Bulka has worked tirelessly on behalf of our community. His acts of kindness, unity and reconciliation continue to serve as an inspiration to all who seek to improve their communities. I support this commemorative naming without reservation,' said City Councillor Jean Cloutier, whose Alta Vista Ward includes the park."

The proposal to rename the park in honour of Rabbi Bulka originated in a Machzikei Hadas committee organizing a celebration of

1. *Ottawa Jewish Bulletin*, 2019.

both the congregation's centennial and Rabbi Bulka's half-century of leadership.

> "'Since coming to Ottawa in 1967, Rabbi Bulka has not stopped helping people regardless of their faith or background,' said the committee co-chair, Bram Bregman, who initiated the idea and led the process to rename the park after Rabbi Bulka. 'Permanently naming a park in honour of Rabbi Bulka is a most fitting way to recognize the kindness he has shown others and to inspire others to do the same.'"
>
> "'I am so delighted that the city park adjacent to the synagogue that Rabbi Bulka led for 50 years will permanently bear his name,' added Ron Prehogan, the committee's other co-chair'. There can be no more deserving honouree than Rabbi Bulka, who has given so much for so many years to the eternal betterment of our community.'"

Bram Bregman, a close family friend of Rabbi Bulka, wrote up the official proposal on behalf of Machzikei Hadas in order to advocate for the renaming of the park on Featherston drive.

> "Ever since moving to Ottawa in 1967, Rabbi Bulka's daily mission is to serve and help every single person in Ottawa. He cares deeply and passionately not only for the members of his congregation or of the Jewish community, but rather for all of his fellow citizens in a way that is truly remarkable and unprecedented. In short, he is the consummate community leader.
>
> Widely respected for his kindness, warmth, activism, wit, and wisdom, Rabbi Bulka is known for always being there to serve the needs and improve the lives of every person regardless of their religion, background, or outlook. Rabbi Bulka has been continuously supporting and enhancing the City of Ottawa for 52 years straight and has no plans to ever stop doing that.
>
> With the full support of the Alta Vista Community Association, we believe the time has come for the City of Ottawa to permanently recognize the remarkable contributions of Rabbi Bulka to the entire national capital region by naming a park in his honour."

Bregman then proceeded to list some of his major contributions, previous roles, and awards. I will attach the list here, so that the reader can have a sense of the breadth of Rabbi Bulka's reach.

## Community Roles

- Chair of the Trillium Gift of Life Network (responsible for all organ and tissue donation in Ontario) since 2006 (role just ended in 2019)
- Founder and Chair of Ottawa Kindness Week in 2008, which continues to this day (and in 2021 became nationalized!)
- Founder of Kind Canada, a national charity based in Ottawa committed to spreading kindness
- Honorary Chaplain of the Dominion Command of the Royal Canadian Legion, Member of the Interfaith Committee on Canadian Military Chaplaincy, and delivers the benediction speech at the National Remembrance Day ceremony at the National War Memorial in Ottawa
- First Vice-Chair of Pallium Canada, a charity based in Ottawa dedicated to improving palliative care in Canada
- Member of Community Advisory Board for Ottawa Integrative Cancer Centre
- Patron of the Ottawa Multifaith Housing Initiative
- Chair of the Ottawa International Airport Multi-Faith Welcoming Committee
- Campaign Chair of Jewish Federation of Ottawa
- Adjunct Professor at Carleton University since 1979
- Chair of the Courage Campaign for the Ottawa Regional Cancer Foundation which raised $25 million for cancer care
- Chair of Bruyere Hospice Ottawa West Campaign that raised $6 million to build a hospice in Canada
- Chair of the Religious Advisory Board, as well as a member of the Board of Directors, for Canadian Blood Services (and has made over 350 donations at Canadian Blood Services in Ottawa and Gatineau!)

- Chair of the Religious Advisory Committee for the United Way/Centraide of Ottawa-Carleton
- Honourary Member, Board of Trustees, Children's Hospital of Eastern Ontario
- Chair of Canadian Christian-Jewish Consultation
- Co-Chair of Canadian Jewish Congress, and Chair of its Religious and Inter-Religious Affairs Committee
- Host of "Sunday Night with Rabbi Bulka" on 580 CFRA
- Regular contributor to "Ask the Religion Experts" in the *Ottawa Citizen*

## Partial List of Awards and Recognitions

- Minister of Veterans Affairs Commendation, awarded posthumously (2021)
- Canadian Forces Medallion for Distinguished Service (2021)
- Community Champion Special Award of Excellence, Canadian Race Relations Foundation (2014)
- Member, Order of Canada (2013)
- Key to the City, City of Ottawa (2010)
- Honourary Doctor of Laws for Community and Humanitarian Service, Carleton University (2006)
- In 2006, the Ottawa Regional Cancer Foundation established The Rabbi Reuven P. Bulka Award in "celebration of the inspirational leadership and dedication of a great community leader"
- Bronfman Medal, Canadian Jewish Congress (2004)
- Inaugural recipient of National Salute Award, Scouts Canada (2001)
- Mayor's Award for Community Service, City of Ottawa (1999)
- Gilbert Greenberg Distinguished Service Award for exemplary service to the Jewish Community of Ottawa, Jewish Federation of Ottawa (1999)
- Beryl Plumptre Award of Excellence, Kidney Foundation of Canada (1998)
- Canada 125 Medal, Government of Canada (1993)

I want to focus on a few of the awards and recognitions that Rabbi Bulka received:

Rabbi Bulka was awarded "The Keys to the City," the highest city honor, by Ottawa's mayor, Larry O'Brien in 2010.

On May 2, 2013, Rabbi Bulka was awarded the Order of Canada "for his dedicated service to the community, notably in promoting interfaith dialogue, health and humanitarian causes".[1]

According to the Governor General of Canada's site, the honor was bestowed because of

> Rabbi Reuven Bulka's dedication and inspiring leadership have enriched the lives of many Canadians. Rabbi of Congregation Machzikei Hadas for more than 45 years, he has also shared his faith and counsel as an author, broadcaster and regular newspaper columnist. A blood donor 345 times, he is best known for his tireless community involvement in interfaith dialogue, health care and humanitarian causes, including the Ottawa Regional Cancer Foundation Courage Campaign, the Trillium Gift of Life Network, and Kindness Week, which he founded.

---

1. Governor General of Canada website, accessed on July 10, 2023, https://www.gg.ca/en.

*Appendix B*

# List of Books written by Rabbi Bulka

*Answers to Questions of the Spirit,* Ottawa, Canada: Ottawa Citizen, 2000.

*As a Tree by the Waters – Pirkey Avoth: Psychological and Philosophical Insights,* New York: Feldheim, 1980, revised editions published as *Chapters of the Sages: A Psychological Commentary on Pirkey Avoth,* Northvale, New Jersey: Jason Aronson, 1993, and *Pirkey Avoth: Psychological and Philosophical Insights,* Northvale, New Jersey: Jason Aronson, 1994.

*Best-Kept Secrets of Judaism,* Southfield, Michigan: Targum Press, 2002.

Bulka, Reuven P., and Rikki Ash. *Honeycombs: the Amidah through the Lens of Rav Yonasan Eybishitz & Rav Yosef Hayyim of Baghdad.* Hoboken, New Jersey: Ktav Publishing House, 2017.

*The Coming Cataclysm: The Orthodox-Reform Rift and the Future of the Jewish People,* Ontario, Canada: Mosaic Press, 1984, 2nd edition, 1986.

*Critical Psychological Issues: Judaic Perspectives,* Lanham, Maryland: University Press of America, 1992.

Editor, *Dimensions of Orthodox Judaism,* Hoboken, New Jersey: Ktav Publishing, 1983.

Editor, *Holocaust Aftermath: Continuing Impact on the Generations,* New York: Human Sciences Press, 1981.

Editor, *Mystics and Medics: A Comparison of Mystical and Psychotherapeutic Encounters,* New York: Human Sciences Press, 1979.

Editor, with Joseph B. Fabry and William S. Sahakian, *Finding Meaning in Life: Logotherapy,* foreword by Viktor E. Frankl, Northvale, New Jersey: Jason Aronson, 1995.

Editor, with Joseph Fabry and William S. Sahakian, *Logotherapy in Action,* Northvale, New Jersey: Jason Aronson, 1979.

Editor, with Moshe Halevi Spero, *A Psychology-Judaism Reader,* Springfield, Illinois: Charles C. Thomas, 1983.

*Fixing Tikkun Olam & Other Essays,* Hoboken, New Jersey: Ktav Publishing, 2021.

*Grieving: Personal Reflections,* Ontario, Canada: Mosaic Press, 2006.

*The Haggadah Connection,* Southfield, Michigan: Targum Press, 2005.

*The Haggadah for Pesah, with Translation and Thematic Commentary,* Jerusalem, Israel: Pri Haaretz Publications, 1985.

*Individual, Family, Community: Judeo-Psychological Perspectives,* Ontario, Canada: Mosaic Press, 1989.

*The Jewish Agenda: An Old-new Look at the Big Picture,* Ottawa, Canada: J. Bulka Verlag, 2011.

*Jewish Divorce Ethics: The Right Way to Say Goodbye,* Ogdensburg, New York: Ivy League Press, 1992.

*Jewish Marriage: A Halakhic Ethic,* Hoboken, New Jersey: Ktav Publishing, 1986. (Republished 2016)

*The Jewish Pleasure Principle,* New York: Human Sciences Press, 1987, revised edition published as *Judaism on Pleasure,* Northvale, New Jersey: Jason Aronson, 1995.

*Judaism on Illness and Suffering,* Northvale, New Jersey: Jason Aronson, 1998.

*Loneliness,* Guidance Center, Toronto, Canada: University of Toronto, 1984.

*Modeh* Ani:Twelve *Magical Words.* Hoboken, New Jersey: Ktav Publishing, 2018.

*Modern Folk Judaism: The Problem and the Challenge,* Hoboken, New Jersey: Ktav Publishing, 2003.

*More Answers to Questions of the Spirit,* Ontario, Canada: Mosaic Press, 2002.

*More of What You Thought You Knew about Judaism: 354 Common*

*Misconceptions about Jewish Life,* Northvale, New Jersey: Jason Aronson, 1993.

*More Torah Therapy: Further Reflections on the Weekly Sidrah and Special Occasions,* Hoboken, New Jersey: Ktav Publishing, 1993.

*Old Ideas for New Times: Opinion Columns & Op Eds from the Ottawa Citizen,* Ottawa, Canada: J. Bulka Verlag, 2013.

*One Man, One Woman, One Lifetime: An Argument for Moral Tradition,* Lafayette, Los Huntington House, 1995.

*Pesach: Its Meaning and Purpose,* Publications Committee, New York: Rabbinical Council of America, 1992.

*Pirkay Avos on Marriage: Timely Ideas from a Timeless Source,* Hoboken, New Jersey: Ktav Publishing, 2020.

*The Quest for Ultimate Meaning: Principles and Applications of Logotherapy,* New York: Philosophical Library, 1979, revised edition published as *Work, Love, Suffering and Death: A Jewish/Psychological Perspective through Logotherapy,* Northvale, New Jersey: Jason Aronson, 1998.

*The* RCA *Life-cycle Madrikh,* New York, NY: Mesorah Publications, 1995.

*Religion from A to Z. Renfrew*: General Store Publishing House, 2006.

*Sermonic Wit,* Jerusalem, Israel: Keren HaYesod, 1995.

*Sex and the Talmud: Reflections on Human Relations,* New York: Peter Pauper Press, 1979.

*Torah Therapy: Reflections on the Weekly Sedra and Special Occasions,* Hoboken, New Jersey: Ktav Publishing, 1983.

*Tefilah v'Tikvah: Prayer and Hope,* Hoboken, NJ: Ktav Publishing, 1997.

*Turning Grief into Gratitude: Reflections and Recommendations on Mourning and Condolence,* Ottawa, Canada: A Paper Spider Production, 2007.

*Uncommon Sense for Common Problems,* Toronto, Canada: Lugus Productions, 1990.

*An Unforgettable Hour: Congregation Machzikei Hadas Receives a Coat of Arms,* Ottawa, Canada: Congregation Machzikei Hadas, 1997.

*What You Thought You Knew about Judaism: 341 Common Misconceptions about Jewish Life,* Northvale, New Jersey: Jason Aronson, 1989.

*The Wit and Wisdom of the Talmud,* New York: Peter Pauper Press, 1974.

*Work, Love, Suffering, Death: A Jewish/Psychological Perspective through Logotherapy*, Northvale, New Jersey: Jason Aronson, 1997.

## PERIODICAL/JOURNAL PUBLICATIONS:

Contributing Editor of "Viewpoints" in *Jewish Spectator.*

Contributing Editor, Section Editor, *Rabbinical Council of America Sermon Manual,* 1977–82.

Contributor to magazines, including *Jewish Digest, Midstream, Jewish Life, Journal of Ecumenical Studies, Journal of Halacha and Contemporary Society,* and *Journal of Humanistic Psychology.*

Editor, *Family and Marriage Newsletter,* 1976–89.

Founder and Editor, *Journal of Psychology and Judaism,* 1976–.

Member of Editorial Advisory Board, *Pastoral Counseling Encyclopedia.*

Member of Editorial Board, *International Forum for Logotherapy, Journal of Religion and Health, Pastoral Psychology,* and *Tradition.*

Opinion column in *Ottawa Citizen,* 1974–78, 1989–.

"The Shiv'ah Visit," New York: Jewish Board of Family and Children's, 1998.

*Appendix C*

# Sabba-isms:

"Closure" – there was no such thing, Rabbi Bulka believed

"Have an easy fast" – "Have a meaningful fast," as Rabbi Bulka would say

"She had a baby" – "She still has a baby," Rabbi Bulka would respond

"I need to kill time" – "Why would you kill time? Time is so precious!"

"I would like to (thank you or wish you a Good Shabbos)" – "Ok, so thank me or wish me a good Shabbos"

"Thanks for being there for me" – "Where is 'there?' Instead, thank you for supporting me, etc."

"Retired" – "changed in status"

"Haman-Tashen" – Rabbi Bulka did not believe in naming the main food of the Purim holiday after the enemy. "Tashen," he would call them (as did the local bakery as per his request).

"Give back" – When you give, you give. Saying that you are giving back implies that you are only giving because you received something in the first place.

"I'm good" – When Rabbi Bulka would ask "how are you", if you would respond "I'm good", he would say "I know you're good. But are you well?"